To our families

EXPLORING
ENGLISH

5

Tim Harris • **Allan Rowe**

LONGMAN

Exploring English 5

Copyright © 1997 by Addison Wesley Longman
All rights reserved.

Text credit: page 152, *Career Sins* reprinted by permission of Ink Inc.

Addison Wesley Longman, 10 Bank Street, White Plains, NY 10606

Editorial Director: Joanne Dresner
Acquisitions Editor: Anne Boynton-Trigg
Production Editors: Thea Mohr, Liza Pleva
Text Design: Curt Belshe, Naomi Ganor
Cover Design: Curt Belshe
Cover Illustration: Allan Rowe
Composition: Kim Teixeira, Kathleen Marks

ISBN 0-201-82579-1
Library of Congress Cataloging-in-Publication Data
Harris, Tim
     Exploring English / Tim Harris; illustrated by Allan Rowe.
          p.   cm.
     1. English language—Textbooks for foreign speakers.   I. Rowe,
Allan.   II. Title.
PE1128.H347   1995
428.2'4—dc20   94-47408
                                                         CIP

     4 5 6 7 8 9 10-CRK-99 98

Contents

Chapter 5   82

TOPICS
Military service
Jobs
Leisure activities
Exercise

GRAMMAR
Had to/will have to
Verb + object + infinitive (with "to")
Would rather

FUNCTIONS
Talking about obligation in the past
   and future
Interviewing for a job
Expressing preference
Making conclusions
Giving opinions

Chapter 6   100

TOPICS
Places to live
Juvenile delinquency
Work

GRAMMAR
Second conditional
So + adjective/such + noun
Reflexive pronouns

FUNCTIONS
Expressing possibility and probability
Making wishes
Talking about consequences
Giving advice
Persuading

Chapter 7   118

TOPICS
Housing
The legal system
Dreams

GRAMMAR
Gerunds

FUNCTIONS
Criticizing
Asking for and giving directions
Telling a story
Describing people
Talking about dreams
Renting an apartment

Chapter 8   137

TOPICS
Leisure activities
Proverbs
Current issues
Problems at work

GRAMMAR
Review

FUNCTIONS
Describing experiences
Making comparisons
Agreeing and disagreeing
Giving reasons
Solving problems
Talking about feelings/emotions
Recommending
Giving opinions

Appendix   158

Irregular verbs
Phrasal verbs
Tapescript

Preface

Exploring English is a comprehensive, six-level course for adult and young adult students of English. It teaches all four language skills—listening, speaking, reading, and writing—with an emphasis on oral communication. The course combines a strong grammar base with in-depth coverage of language functions and life skills.

Exploring English:

Teaches grammar inductively. The basic structures are introduced in context through illustrated situations and dialogues. Students use the structures in talking about the situations and re-enacting the dialogues. They encounter each structure in a variety of contexts, including practice exercises, pair work activities, and readings. This repeated exposure enables students to make reliable and useful generalizations about the language. They develop a "language sense"—a feeling for words—that carries over into their daily use of English.

Includes language functions in every chapter from beginning through advanced levels. Guided conversations, discussions, and role plays provide varied opportunities to practice asking for and giving information, expressing likes and dislikes, agreeing and disagreeing, and so on.

Develops life skills in the areas most important to students: food, clothing, transportation, work, housing, and health care. Everyday life situations provide contexts for learning basic competencies: asking directions, taking a bus, buying food, shopping for clothes, and so on. Students progress from simpler tasks, such as describing occupations at the beginning level, to interviewing for jobs and discussing problems at work at more advanced levels.

Incorporates problem solving and critical thinking in many of the lessons, especially at the intermediate and advanced levels. The stories in *Exploring English* present a cast of colorful characters who get involved in all kinds of life problems, ranging from personal relationships to work-related issues and politics. Students develop critical-thinking skills as they discuss these problems, give their opinions, and try to find solutions. These discussions also provide many opportunities for students to talk about their own lives.

Provides extensive practice in listening comprehension through illustrated situations. Students are asked to describe each illustration in their own words before listening to the accompanying story (which appears on the reverse side of the page). Then they answer questions based on the story, while looking at the illustration. The students respond to what they see and hear without referring to a text, just as they would in actual conversation.

Offers students frequent opportunities for personal expression. The emphasis throughout *Exploring English* is on communication—encouraging students to use the language to express their own ideas and feelings. Free-response questions in

Books 1 and 2 give students the opportunity to talk about themselves using simple, straightforward English. Every chapter in Books 3–6 has a special section, called "One Step Further," that includes discussion topics such as work, leisure activities, cinema, travel, dating, and marriage. Ideas for role plays are also provided to give additional opportunities for free expression. The general themes are familiar to students because they draw on material already covered in the same chapter. Role plays give students a chance to interact spontaneously— perhaps the most important level of practice in developing communication skills.

Provides continuous review and reinforcement. Each chapter concludes with a review section, and every fourth chapter is devoted entirely to review, allowing students to practice newly acquired language in different combinations.

Presents attractive art that visually supports and is integral with the language being taught. Humorous and imaginative illustrations, in full color, make *Exploring English* fun for students. In addition, the richness of the art allows teachers to devise their own spin-off activities, increasing the teachability of each page.

Levels 1–4 of *Exploring English* are accompanied by Workbooks. The Workbook lessons are closely coordinated with the lessons in the Student Book. They provide additional writing practice using the same grammatical structures and vocabulary while expanding on basic functions and life skills. The activities range from sentence-completion exercises to guided paragraph and composition writing.

Student Books and Workbooks include clear labels and directions for each activity. In addition, Teacher's Resource Manuals are available for each level. These Manuals provide step-by-step guidance for teaching each page, expansion activities, and answers to the exercises. Each student page is reproduced for easy reference.

Audiocassettes for each level featuring an entertaining variety of native voices round out the series.

Chapter 1

TOPICS
Politics
Meeting people
Movies

GRAMMAR
Present perfect continuous
Verb + gerund
Gerund as subject

FUNCTION
Talking about things people have been doing
Expressing likes and dislikes
Giving opinions
Telling a story
Predicting

1

2

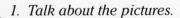
1. *Talk about the pictures.*
2. *Listen to the stories.*
3. *Answer the story questions.*

READING

1 Mr. Bascomb would like to be the next mayor of Wickam City. He has been running for office since last year. As a banker, Mr. Bascomb is concerned about the economy. He wants to bring more business to the city and has promised to build a toy factory in City Park. Mr. Bascomb has been making a lot of speeches lately. He has been talking to the voters about jobs, taxes, and crime. Mr. Bascomb has been spending a lot of money on his election campaign. So far, it has cost him over $50,000.

1. How long has Mr. Bascomb been running for mayor?
2. How does he plan to help the economy of Wickam City?
3. Has Mr. Bascomb been spending a lot of money to win the election?
4. How much has he spent so far?

2 Otis Jackson is also running for mayor of Wickam City. He has been campaigning for a few months. As an artist, Otis appreciates the natural beauty of Wickam City. He wants to protect the environment and has promised to save City Park. Otis is concerned about ordinary working people. He has been asking questions and listening to people's complaints about city government. Otis has very little money to spend on his campaign, but he has a lot of volunteers and they have been working hard for him.

1. How long has Otis been campaigning?
2. Is he more concerned about the economy or the environment?
3. What has Otis promised to do about City Park?
4. How is Otis's campaign different from Mr. Bascomb's campaign?

PRESENT PERFECT CONTINUOUS: Affirmative	
Otis has been working hard.	They have been working hard.
He _____ .	You _____ .
Suzi _____ .	We _____ .
She _____ .	I _____ .

WRITTEN EXERCISE • *Complete the sentences using the present perfect continuous.*

Mr. Bascomb *has been making* a lot of speeches lately. (make)

The volunteers *have been working* hard for Otis. (work)

1. Albert _____ at the university for two years now. (study)

2. He _____ a car since he was sixteen. (drive)

3. We _____ some beautiful weather this month. (have)

4. Linda _____ a lot of time at the beach. (spend)

5. I _____ some letters to my family. (write)

6. You _____ too much television. (watch)

7. Our basketball team _____ a lot of games. (win)

8. The boys _____ hard this year. (play)

Listen and practice.

Suzi Suzuki, star reporter for the Wickam Daily News, *is interviewing Otis Jackson about his campaign for mayor.*

SUZI: Mr. Jackson, what is the most important issue in this campaign?

OTIS: The quality of life in Wickam City. We haven't been doing enough to protect the environment.

SUZI: Can you give an example?

OTIS: Sure. The opposition wants to build a large toy factory in City Park. But I say we need the park more than we need a new factory.

SUZI: Mr. Bascomb says you're too inexperienced to be mayor. He says you've never held public office.

OTIS: Neither has he. At least I've been talking to the people and trying to understand their problems.

SUZI: Mr. Bascomb has been spending a lot of money on his campaign. Does that worry you?

OTIS: No, not really. You can't win the election with money alone.

SUZI: Are you satisfied with your campaign so far?

OTIS: Yes, I am. The people have been giving me a lot of support. They're wonderful.

SUZI: Your volunteer workers are very impressive. I don't think you have anything to worry about.

OTIS: Neither do I. But it's up to the voters. We'll see.

PRACTICE 1 • *Imagine you are Mr. Bascomb. Tell what you have been doing to win the election.*

1. make/speeches
   I've been making a lot of speeches.

2. hold/meetings

3. give/interviews

4. talk to/voters

5. shake/hands

6. kiss/babies

7. make/promises

8. hire/campaign workers

9. buy/advertisements

PRACTICE 2 • *Talk about Mr. Bascomb. What has he been doing to win the election?*

PRACTICE 3 • *In addition to Mr. Jackson and Mr. Bascomb, there is a third candidate for mayor: Mr. Farley. So far, he hasn't been trying very hard to win the election. Imagine you are Mr. Farley. Make negative sentences about your campaign.*

1. make/speeches **I haven't been making many speeches.**

PRACTICE 4 • *Talk about Mr. Farley. What has he been doing wrong?*

1

2

1. *Talk about the pictures.*
2. *Listen to the stories.*
3. *Answer the story questions.*

READING

1 Anne Jones has been working at City Bank for two years. Her boss is Mr. Bascomb. She thinks he is a difficult man and doesn't like working for him. Anne hates typing because it's so boring. And she can't stand taking orders. She avoids talking to Mr. Bascomb as much as possible. "I can't go on doing this work," says Anne. "It's driving me crazy." Anne is happiest when she is away from the job. She loves singing and playing the guitar. Music is the most important thing in her life.

1. How long has Anne been working at City Bank?
2. Why doesn't Anne like working for Mr. Bascomb?
3. Why does she hate typing?
4. What does Anne say about her work?
5. What's the most important thing in Anne's life?
6. What does she love doing?

2 Barbara Martinoli also works at City Bank. She has been working there a little longer than Anne. Barbara and Anne are good friends, but they have different attitudes about their jobs. Barbara really enjoys working at the bank. She respects Mr. Bascomb and doesn't mind taking orders from him. If Barbara wanted to, she could work with her husband, Tino, at the Martinoli Restaurant. But Barbara prefers working at the bank. "I like it here," she says. "I'm learning a lot, and I have a good future."

1. Who's been working at the bank longer, Anne or Barbara?
2. Do they have the same attitude about their jobs?
3. How does Barbara feel about working at the bank?
4. Could Barbara work somewhere else if she wanted to?
5. Why does she prefer working at the bank?

VERB + GERUND: Affirmative	VERB + GERUND: Negative
I enjoy taking the bus.	They don't mind working at night.
__ like _____ .	____ don't enjoy _____ .
__ avoid _____ .	____ don't like _____ .
__ hate _____ .	____ can't stand _____ .

PRACTICE • *Talk about what you like and dislike, using the verb + gerund form.*

take orders
I don't mind taking orders.
OR **I avoid taking orders.**
OR **I can't stand taking orders.**

1. spend money
2. listen to music
3. do homework
4. study at night
5. get up early
6. take the bus
7. go to the market
8. make dinner
9. eat fried food
10. wash the dishes

Listen and practice.

Anne regrets the day she started working at the bank.

ANNE: I can't stand it, Barbara. This work is so boring. What should I do?

BARBARA: You should stop complaining. This job is better than most jobs.

ANNE: You keep telling me that. But it's the same thing every day. I never get a chance to do anything interesting.

BARBARA: Have you told Mr. Bascomb how you feel?

ANNE: No. I avoid talking to him. Besides, he's too busy running for mayor.

BARBARA: Listen. I get along pretty well with Mr. Bascomb. I'll talk to him for you.

ANNE: Don't waste your time. Mr. Bascomb only understands business. He doesn't care about people's feelings.

BARBARA: I don't think you're being fair, Anne.

ANNE: Oh, you're always defending Mr. Bascomb. It was silly of me to ask you for advice.

BARBARA: Take it easy. I'm only trying to help.

ANNE: I'm sorry. I don't mean to be unpleasant. It's just that . . . .

BARBARA: Cheer up, Anne. Everything will turn out all right.

• *Express your feelings about the activities or daily routines in the pictures, using the verb + gerund form.*

1. cooking
A: **I love cooking. How about you?**
B: **I love it, too.**
   OR **I hate it.**

2. shopping
A: **I don't like shopping. How about you?**
B: **I don't like it, either.**
   OR **I enjoy it.**

3. doing housework
A: **I avoid doing housework. How about you?**
B: **I avoid it, too.**
   OR **I don't mind it.**

4. getting up early

5. taking the bus

6. standing in line

7. dancing

8. eating alone

9. kissing in public

10. writing letters

11. exercising

12. washing the dishes

Barney Field has been driving a taxi for several years. He enjoys his work because it gives him a chance to meet a lot of interesting people. Last week, for example, he met a famous movie star at the airport. It was Ula Hackey, Barney's favorite actress. He recognized her as soon as she got in the taxi.

"Please take me to the Plaza Hotel," she said. "And don't waste any time."

"Yes, ma'am," said Barney. He turned around and smiled at her. "Aren't you Miss Ula Hackey, the famous actress?"

"That's right," she said. "I suppose you've seen me in the movies."

"I sure have," said Barney. "I've seen all of your pictures. I'm a real fan of yours."

Barney started telling Miss Hackey how much he enjoyed her pictures. He thought she was the best actress in the world. Miss Hackey was very flattered. She enjoyed listening to Barney and thought he was very pleasant.

"You're quite a guy," she said. "What's your name?"

"Barney Field. At your service."

"You know, Barney," she went on, "you're different from most people I meet. Almost everyone is afraid to talk to me because I'm a big star. But it doesn't seem to bother you at all."

"Well, I am a little nervous," said Barney. "But in my work I meet all kinds of people, and I enjoy talking."

"Don't stop now," said Miss Hackey. "Tell me about yourself. You seem like a very interesting person."

Barney was overjoyed. He loved talking about himself and made the most of his opportunity. He started telling Miss Hackey about his experiences as a taxi driver. His favorite story was about a man who didn't have any money and tried to pay his fare with cigars.

Miss Hackey just sat back and listened. It was fascinating. After a while she leaned forward and said, "Barney, you enjoy telling stories, don't you?"

"Yes, ma'am. I've been telling stories ever since I was a little boy."

"Well, I hope you've got a good one for the police officer right behind us."

Barney looked out the window and saw a police officer on a motorcycle. The officer signaled for Barney to pull over to the side of the road.

"Didn't you see the light back there?" asked the officer.

Barney shook his head. "What light, officer?"

"The stop light at the intersection. You went right through it."

Barney was very embarrassed. He started to say something, but he couldn't find the words. Miss Hackey leaned forward and whispered in his ear, "If you don't mind, Barney, I'll do the talking." Then she turned and looked at the officer, who didn't seem to recognize her. "It wasn't the driver's fault," she said. "He wasn't responsible. You see . . ."

"Of course it was his fault," interrupted the officer. "He was doing the driving! I'm going to have to give you a ticket," he said to Barney. The police officer wrote out the ticket, handed it to the driver, and rode away on his motorcycle. Barney looked very unhappy.

"Cheer up," said Miss Hackey. "I'll pay the ticket for you."

"Oh, that's very generous of you," said Barney. "But I can't accept. After all, I was doing the driving."

"Well, maybe you can accept another offer."

"What's that?" said Barney.

"I've just started making a new movie," said Miss Hackey. "We're looking for someone who can play the part of a taxi driver. Would you like to do it?"

"Of course!" said Barney. He felt better already. "I've always wanted to be in the movies. Now's my chance."

STORY QUESTIONS

1. How did Barney meet Ula Hackey?
2. Why was he so happy to meet her?
3. What did Ula Hackey think of Barney?
4. How was he different from most people she met?
5. What was Barney's favorite story about?
6. Why did the police officer stop Barney?
7. Why do you think Barney didn't see the stop light?
8. Did the police officer give Barney a ticket or just a friendly warning?
9. How did Miss Hackey try to help Barney?
10. Why didn't Barney accept?
11. What was Miss Hackey's second offer?
12. What was Barney's reaction?
13. Do you think this was a good day or a bad day for Barney? Why?

READER'S THEATER • *Three students play the parts of Barney, Ula Hackey, and the police officer. A fourth student is the narrator. Read dramatically from the story.*

PRACTICE 1 • *Change the sentences using gerunds.*

> It's dangerous to drive fast.
> **Driving fast is dangerous.**
>
> It's stupid to waste time.
> **Wasting time is stupid.**

1. It's expensive to eat out.
2. It's difficult to save money.
3. It's economical to take the bus.
4. It's important to help others.
5. It's wonderful to make new friends.
6. It's fantastic to be in love.
7. It's difficult to be a good loser.
8. It's easy to ride a bicycle.
9. It's fun to dance.

PRACTICE 2 • *Complete the sentences with appropriate adjectives. There can be more than one appropriate adjective for each sentence.*

> Saving money is **smart.**
> OR Saving money is **difficult.**

1. Finding a good job is . . .
2. Working for free is . . .
3. Planning for the future is . . .
4. Doing the same thing every day is . . .
5. Listening to music is . . .
6. Learning English is . . .
7. Calling long distance is . . .
8. Driving a small car is . . .
9. Walking the streets at night is . . .

WRITTEN EXERCISE • *Complete the sentences using gerunds.*

He enjoys *listening to the radio.*

We've finished *painting the apartment.*

1. She likes _____

2. They've started _____

3. He can't stand _____

4. I don't mind _____

5. We've stopped _____

6. You don't like _____

7. She avoids _____

PAIR WORK • *Have conversations similar to the examples. Student B uses **so** or **neither** to show agreement with Student A.*

A: I'm going to study tonight.

A: I haven't done my homework yet.

B: **So am I.**

B: **Neither have I.**

1. A: I'd like a cup of coffee.   B: _____ .
2. A: I don't watch TV very much.   B: _____ .
3. A: I went shopping yesterday.   B: _____ .
4. A: I'm tired.   B: _____ .
5. A: I couldn't sleep last night.   B: _____ .
6. A: I won't be here Saturday.   B: _____ .
7. A: I have a lot of things to do.   B: _____ .
8. A: I've always been very busy.   B: _____ .
9. A: I'm never bored.   B: _____ .

GROUP WORK • *Tell how you feel about these activities. Find out what you have in common with the others.*

get up early	do homework	shop	cook
take the bus	listen to rock music	write letters	wash the dishes
come to class	watch TV news	talk about politics	do housework

A: **I enjoy cooking.**
B: **So do I. I think it's fun.**
C: **Not me. I hate cooking. What about you?**
D: **I don't mind cooking.**

Use these expressions:

I enjoy/hate/don't mind . . . -ing.
So do I./Neither do I.
Me too./Not me.

PAIR WORK • *Ask and answer questions about the pictures.*

1. Suzi
A: **What has Suzi been doing?**
B: **She's been picking flowers.**

2. Otis and Gloria
A: **What have Otis and Gloria been doing?**
B: **They've been riding bicycles.**

3. Barbara and Tino

4. Nick

5. Peter and Maria

6. Linda

7. Fred

8. Cathy and Danny

Movies are the most popular form of entertainment for millions of Americans. They go to the movies to escape their normal everyday existence and to experience a life more exciting than their own. They may choose to see a particular film because they like the actors or because they've heard the film has a good story. But the main reason people go to the movies is to escape. Sitting in a dark theater, watching the images on the screen, they enter another world that is very real to them. They become involved in the lives of the characters in the movie, and for two hours they forget all about their own problems. They are in a dream world where things often appear to be more romantic and beautiful than in real life.

The biggest "dream factories" are in Hollywood, the capital of the film industry. Each year, Hollywood studios make hundreds of movies that are shown all over the world. People everywhere have seen the films of Charlie Chaplin, Humphrey Bogart, Marilyn Monroe, and more recently, Arnold Schwarzenegger and Tom Hanks. American movies are popular because they tell interesting stories and are well made. They provide the public with heroes who do things the average person would like to do but often can't. People have to cope with many problems and frustrations in real life, so they get a lift when they see the "good guys" win in the movies.

Hollywood producers are usually not as successful as the heroes in their movies. It's hard for them to predict what the movie-going public will want to see a year from now. In fact, seven times out of ten, producers are unsuccessful and their movies lose money. Since the average Hollywood movie costs $30 million to make, a picture that "bombs" at the box office can be a disaster for the producer. Making movies is obviously a very expensive and risky business. But it's also an exciting and glamorous business, and there's always the chance of producing a blockbuster like *Jurassic Park*.

Hollywood produces many different kinds of films, including mysteries, comedies, musicals, love stories, and horror films. As different as these films may be, they generally have one thing in common: conflict. The main character, or protagonist, wants something very badly and will do anything to get it. The antagonist tries to stop the protagonist from achieving his goal. This opposition creates conflict, and conflict is the heart of drama. To give an example, let's say the protagonist is a young man from the wrong side of the tracks who wants to marry the beautiful daughter of a rich banker. The father thinks the young man is unworthy of his daughter, and he forbids her to see him. The young man, who is very much in love, refuses to give up without a fight. The conflict between the young man and the girl's father is what makes the story interesting: it forces the main characters to take action, and through their actions we see them as they really are. In a good story, the protagonist changes—he is not the same at the end of the story as he was at the beginning. He learns something from his experiences that makes him a different, perhaps better, person. And we learn something from watching him. Good movies not only entertain us, they also help us understand a little more about life.

1. Why do people go to the movies?
2. Why are American movies popular?
3. Who are some famous Hollywood stars?
4. Why do we need movie heroes?
5. Is making movies a risky business? Why?
6. What kinds of movies are made in Hollywood?
7. Why is conflict necessary in a movie?
8. What creates conflict? Give an example of conflict.
9. What happens to the main character in a good movie?
10. What can we learn from movies?

FREE RESPONSE

1. What kinds of movies do you like?
2. Do you prefer moves with happy endings?
3. What is the best movie you have seen this year? Why do you like it?
4. What is your favorite movie of all time? What was it about?
5. Who are your favorite movie stars? Why do you like them?
6. Would you like to work in the movies? If so, would you rather be an actor, a director, or a producer?
7. Do you think Hollywood movies give a true picture of life in the United States?
8. What impressions do you get about Americans from the movies?
9. What is your opinion of American movies? Do you have any complaints or suggestions?
10. Do you think there's too much sex and violence in the movies?
11. Do you think censorship is sometimes necessary? Why?
12. Do you think movies have a good influence, a bad influence, or no influence on society?

GROUP WORK • *Tell the story of the young man (James), the young woman (Susan), and her father (Mr. Graves). One student describes the first picture, another student describes the second picture, and so on.*

A: The story begins at the gas station, where James works. At the moment, James is . . .

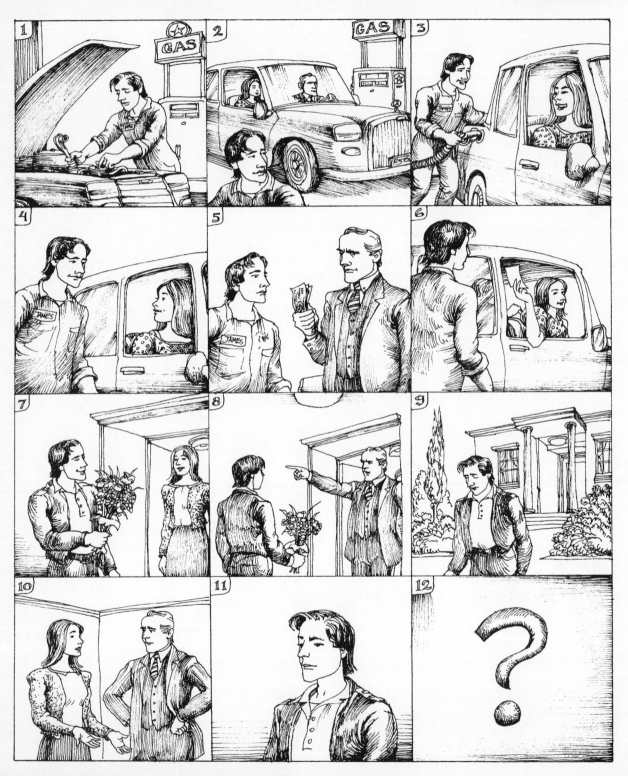

CLASS ACTIVITY • *What happens after Mr. Graves forbids his daughter to see James? How do you think the story ends?*

TALKING ABOUT POLITICS

Mr. Jackson and Mr. Bascomb are both running for mayor of Wickam City. The mayor is the most powerful person in city government and makes decisions that affect the lives of all the residents.

1. Who is the most important government official in your city?
2. How often are there elections?
3. How do the candidates try to get votes?
4. What do you think is the most serious problem in your city? What should the people do about it?
5. Do you talk about politics with your family and friends? Do you share the same opinions? Explain.

GROUP WORK • *Make a list of the main problems in your city. Discuss these problems and decide which one you think is the most serious. Share your finding with the class.*

TALKING ABOUT MEETING PEOPLE

Last week Barney had a chance meeting with a famous movie star. It was quite an experience for him.

1. Have you ever met a famous person? When? Where? How?
2. What famous person would you most like to meet? Why?
3. Do you enjoy meeting new people? Is it easy or difficult to meet people where you live?
4. Where and how do people usually meet?
5. What are some things people say when they want to start a conversation with a person they don't know?

ROLE PLAY

Student A plays a taxi driver. Student B plays a famous person who has just arrived in town.

Situation 1: The taxi driver stops to give the person a ride. The driver gets very excited when he discovers that his passenger is famous, and he starts asking a lot of questions.

Situation 2: The passenger asks the taxi driver questions about the city. She wants to know about restaurants, entertainment, and interesting places to visit.

COMPOSITION

1. Describe how you met an important person in your life. When and where did it happen? What were the circumstances?
2. Describe your favorite movie. When and where did the story take place? What was it about?
3. Write a short composition about the picture story on page 18. Add your own ending.

VOCABULARY

advertisement	environment	keep (v.)	reaction	taste (n.)
advice	examination		recent	ticket (n.)
appreciate	example	lately	recognize	
attitude		likeable	regret (v.)	unpleasant
avoid	fair (adj.)	love (n.)	responsible	
	fan (n.)			voter
boring (adj.)	fascinating (adj.)	most (n.)	satisfied	
boss (n.)	fault		satisfy (v.)	waste (v.)
bother (v.)	flatter (v.)	opportunity	shake (v.)	whisper (v.)
	forbid		silly	
campaign (n.)		protect	speech	
campaign (v.)	inexperienced		stop light	
candidate	interrupt	quality	support (n.)	
complain	intersection		support (v.)	
concern (n.)	interview (n.)		suppose	
	interview (v.)			
defend	issue (n.)			
ear				
economy				
election				
embarrass				

EXPRESSIONS

I can't stand it.	If you don't mind.	You're quite a guy.
It's driving me crazy.	Don't waste your time.	Everything will turn out all right.
We'll see.	Cheer up.	I get along well with him.
It's up to the voters.	Take it easy.	He made the most of his opportunity.
Me too.	to be concerned	at least
Not me.	to be satisfied	as soon as
	to be embarrassed	at your service

GRAMMAR SUMMARY

PRESENT PERFECT

He's spent a lot of money.
She's written some letters.
We've called Mr. Bascomb several times.

PRESENT PERFECT CONTINUOUS

He's She's We've	been	spending a lot of money recently. writing letters all afternoon. calling him since ten o'clock.

Interrogative

How long	has	he been working at the hospital? she been living in Wickam City?
	have	you been studying English? they been watching television?

PRESENT PERFECT CONTINUOUS with FOR and SINCE

He's She's	been	working at the hospital living in Wickam City	for	two years. a long time.
I've They've		studying English watching television	since	last summer. five o'clock.

Negative

He She	hasn't	been	listening to the radio.
I They	haven't		going to the park.

VERB + GERUND

They	love hate started stopped avoid enjoy prefer don't mind don't like can't stand	taking the bus. working at night.

GERUND as SUBJECT

Dancing Driving fast Taking the bus	is	fun. dangerous. economical.

Chapter

T O P I C S

Leisure activities

Gripes

Weddings

Children

Marriage

G R A M M A R

First conditional

Defining relative clauses with "whose" and "where"

Noun clauses

F U N C T I O N S

Expressing probability

Asking for and giving information

Expressing dissatisfaction

Persuading

1

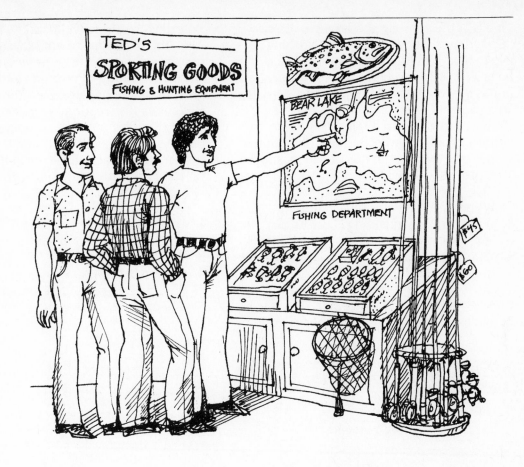

2

1. *Talk about the pictures.*
2. *Listen to the stories.*
3. *Answer the story questions.*

READING

1 Tino is at the sporting goods store with two of his friends. They are planning a fishing trip to Bear Lake this weekend. There has been a lot of rain recently, so everyone hopes the weather will be good on Saturday. If the weather is good, Tino will go fishing with his friends. But if it rains, he'll stay home and help his wife, Barbara. She wants to paint the living room this weekend, and Tino promised to help her.

1. Where are Tino and his friends?
2. What are they planning?
3. What's the weather been like recently?
4. What does Barbara want to do this weekend?
5. Did Tino promise to help Barbara?
6. What will Tino do if it rains?
7. What will he do if the weather is good?

2 Peter is a world traveler, and a ladies' man, too. He loves to visit foreign countries and go out with beautiful women. Although Peter has a lot of girlfriends, he has never gotten married. He enjoys his freedom as a bachelor. If Peter does get married some day, he will have to stop traveling so much. But if he remains a bachelor, he will keep on traveling and going out with beautiful women.

1. What does Peter love to do?
2. Has he ever been married?
3. What does Peter enjoy as a bachelor?
4. What will happen if he gets married?
5. What will happen if he remains a bachelor?

FIRST CONDITIONAL*

If it rains, he'll stay home.

_____ , _____ help his wife.

_____ , _____ do some work.

_____ , _____ paint the living room.

The if-clause states an action that can really happen. If the action in the if-clause happens, it is quite possible that the action in the result clause will happen. We use the first conditional to talk about what might happen in the future.

PRACTICE • *Complete the sentences.*

Tino wants to go fishing. If it's a nice day, **he'll go fishing.**

He promised to help Barbara. If it rains, **he'll help Barbara.**

1. Anne would like to learn Spanish. If she goes to Mexico, . . .
2. Mr. Bascomb hopes to build a factory in City Park. If he becomes mayor, . . .
3. Otis promised to save the park. If he becomes mayor, . . .
4. Jimmy and Linda want to go to the beach. If it's a nice day, . . .
5. Jack wants to buy a new car. If he gets the money, . . .
6. Mrs. Brown promised to get some tomatoes. If she goes to the market, . . .
7. I would like to visit the Art Museum. If I have time, . . .
8. My friends would like to watch television. If they go home, . . .
9. Fred is trying to find a job. If he keeps trying, . . .

*In English there are three types of conditional sentences. For convenience we refer to them as first, second, and third conditional.

Listen and practice.

PETER: What are you doing this weekend, Tino?

TINO: It depends on the weather. If it's a nice day, I'll go fishing at Bear Lake.

PETER: What if it rains?

TINO: If it rains, I'll stay home and paint the living room.

PETER: I'll bet it was Barbara's idea to paint the living room. Is she going to help you?

TINO: She'll help me if I ask her. But I'm hoping the weather will be good so I can go to Bear Lake.

PETER: I hear it's a beautiful place. If you go fishing, will you take your camera?

TINO: Sure. But I won't take any pictures unless I catch some really big fish.

PETER: How is the fishing now?

TINO: It should be excellent. Do you want to come, Peter?

PETER: Sure, I'm always free on the weekends.

TINO: Hmm. I guess that's one advantage of being a bachelor.

CLASS ACTIVITY 1 • *What are the people doing in pictures 1 and 2? What are some other things you can do on a sunny day?*

CLASS ACTIVITY 2 • *What are the people doing in pictures 3 and 4? What are some other things you can do on a rainy day?*

PAIR WORK • *Talk about your plans for Sunday.*

    A: What are you going to do on Sunday?

    B: Well, if it's a nice day, I'll _____ .

    A: What if it rains?

    B: If it rains, I'll stay home and _____ .

Listen and practice.

JENNY: Marty, let's play a game. See if you can guess what I'm thinking of.

MARTY: Okay. Go ahead.

JENNY: I'm thinking of a man whose favorite pastime is chasing butterflies.

MARTY: That's easy. Dr. Pasto.

JENNY: I'm thinking of a woman whose house is full of cats.

MARTY: That must be Mrs. Golo.

JENNY: Now I'm thinking of a place where people have picnics.

MARTY: I know. City Park.

JENNY: I'm thinking of a restaurant where you can have great ice cream.

MARTY: That must be the Martinoli Restaurant.

JENNY: Very good, Marty. You guessed them all. Can you guess what I want to do now?

MARTY: Sure, you want to have ice cream at the Martinoli Restaurant. Let's go.

THE RELATIVE PRONOUN **WHOSE**

We know a man whose daughter is getting married.

_____ whose son is going to the university.

_____ whose wife works at the airport.

_____ whose job is selling encyclopedias.

PRACTICE • _Combine the sentences using **whose**._

I'm thinking of a man. His favorite pastime is chasing butterflies.
I'm thinking of a man <u>whose</u> favorite pastime is chasing butterflies.

We saw a woman. Her dog was bigger than she was.
We saw a woman <u>whose</u> dog was bigger than she was.

1. I talked to a boy. His father is a salesman.
2. He works for a woman. Her only interest is making money.
3. We know a girl. Her brother lives in France.
4. They have a friend. His family is very rich.
5. We heard about a man. His favorite pastime is eating.
6. He married a woman. Her favorite pastime is cooking.
7. I'm thinking of a girl. Her eyes are different colors.
8. She's going out with a boy. His family comes from New York.

THE RELATIVE PRONOUN **WHERE**

That's the place where we met.

_____ where you lost your wallet.

_____ where she had the accident.

_____ where I bought my umbrella.

PAIR WORK • _Have conversations similar to the example._

A: You can have good ice cream _at the Martinoli Restaurant._*
B: I know another place where you can have good ice cream.

A: Where?
B: _At Mom's Cafe._*

*Students name local places.

1. A: You can have picnics . . .
2. A: You can play basketball . . .
3. A: You can see good movies . . .
4. A: You can hear good music . . .
5. A: You can have a good time . . .
6. A: You can meet interesting people . . .
7. A: You can get a job . . .
8. A: You can buy nice shoes . . .

Listen and practice.

FRED: Hi, Nick. Have you seen Barney?

NICK: Yes, he was here this morning.

FRED: Do you know where he went?

NICK: The Plaza Hotel. He went to see Ula Hackey, the famous movie star.

FRED: Ula Hackey? I didn't know she was in Wickam City. I wonder what she's doing here.

NICK: Barney says she came for a little rest. She likes the peace and quiet of our town.

FRED: Oh, I see. Do you know how Barney met her?

NICK: He picked her up at the airport a few days ago.

FRED: Why did he go to see her at the hotel?

NICK: Well, according to Barney, she has a part for him in her new movie.

FRED: I wonder why she wants Barney. He's never had any acting experience.

NICK: It isn't necessary. He's going to play the role of a taxi driver.

FRED: Hmm. I wonder if she needs someone like me.

NICK: You never know, Fred. Anything is possible.

QUESTIONS	NOUN CLAUSES
What is Miss Hackey doing here?	I wonder **what Miss Hackey is doing here.**
How did Barney meet her?	Can you tell me **how Barney met her?**
Is she staying at the Plaza Hotel?	Do you know **if she's staying at the Plaza Hotel?**
When will she make her next movie?	I wonder **when she'll make her next movie.**
Does she have a part for Barney?	Do you know **if she has a part for Barney?**

When questions become noun clauses, use normal word order instead of question word order. When a *yes/no* question becomes a noun clause, use **if** to introduce the noun clause. Do not use **do, does,** or **did** in noun clauses.

WRITTEN EXERCISE • *Complete the sentences using noun clauses.*

Who is that man? Do you know _who that man is ?_

Does he need any help? I wonder _if he needs any help._

1. How much does this book cost? Can you tell me _____

2. What did you say? I didn't hear _____

3. Are they coming to the party? I wonder _____

4. Do we have their phone number? I'm not sure _____

5. How does this machine work? Could you explain _____

6. Where did I leave the key? I can't remember _____

7. Why are you so upset? I don't understand _____

8. Is something wrong? Please tell me _____

9. Did anyone call the police? Do you know _____

PAIR WORK • *Ask your partner questions beginning with Do you know . . . ?*

> Where is the nearest post office?
> A: **Do you know where the nearest post office is?**
> B: **Yes. It's on Bond Street.**
>   OR **I'm not sure. I think there's one on Franklin Avenue.**
>   OR **Sorry. I have no idea.**

1. Where is the nearest library?
2. Is the library open on Saturday?
3. Does the teacher have a dictionary?
4. What does the word "bachelor" mean?
5. Where can I get some envelopes?
6. When does the post office close?
7. How much does an airmail stamp cost?

Today Mr. Bascomb made an important speech at the Wickam Town Hall. He discussed the main issues of the current election campaign. A large number of people turned out to hear him. He seemed relaxed and confident as he spoke to the crowd.

"Ladies and gentlemen," said Mr. Bascomb. "I want to thank you for being here this afternoon. As you know, I'm running for Mayor of Wickam City. In a couple of minutes, I'm going to explain where I stand on the issues. But first, let me tell you a little about myself. I'm a native son of Wickam City. This is where I was born and this is where I grew up. I went to Wickam High School and graduated from Wickam State University, where I met my lovely wife, Henrietta."

At that point, Mr. Bascomb turned around and motioned to his wife, who was sitting behind him on the stage. She was there whenever her husband made a campaign speech. Mrs. Bascomb went to the microphone and urged everyone to vote for her husband. "He's the best person for the job," said Mrs. Bascomb. She was very sincere, and most of the people in the audience seemed to like her. Mr. Bascomb was proud of his wife and happy she could help him with the campaign.

However, Mr. Bascomb wasn't smiling as he returned to the microphone. "My friends," he said. "these are difficult times. There are serious problems facing Wickam City, and we have to do something about them. My opponent is always talking about protecting the environment. But that's not the main issue in this campaign. What's important is jobs and taxes. Many of our people are unemployed, and the cost of government is going up every day. The economy of Wickam City is in bad shape and it's getting worse.

"This can't go on," said Mr. Bascomb. "We have to take action. As president of City Bank, I have had a great deal of business experience, and I know how to manage our city's economy. Ladies and gentlemen, there is only one answer to our problems, and the answer is simple. We need more business in Wickam City. That's why I favor the construction of a toy factory in City Park. A new factory will provide more jobs and tax money.

"My opponent, Mr. Jackson, says we should not build a factory in City Park. He wants to keep the park as it is. I understand his feelings, and maybe some of you agree with him. But let me ask you this: Does Mr. Jackson know another place where we can build a toy factory? The answer, ladies and gentlemen, is no. City Park is the only suitable location. And, for your information, it won't be necessary to use all of the park, only half of it. That way we can still use the park for picnics and other activities.

"Some people, including Mr. Jackson, say we can do without a new toy factory. But they aren't being realistic. Unless we encourage new business in our city, we will have more unemployment and higher taxes. I don't think Mr. Jackson and his followers realize how serious these problems are. Ladies and gentlemen, time is running out! The owners of the toy company want to build their factory as soon as possible. Unless we give them permission to use City Park, they'll build their factory in another city.

"My opponent doesn't care if we lose the factory. But I'd like to know where he is going to get the money to build the new schools and roads we need. How is he going to pay for the high cost of government?

"My friends, I've known Mr. Jackson for years, and I think he is a fine man. But he is too inexperienced to be mayor of Wickam City. You need a man of action with plans for the future. That is why you should elect me as your next mayor. I am sure you will make the right decision. Thank you, ladies and gentlemen."

STORY QUESTIONS

1. What happened today at the Wickam Town Hall?
2. Why did Mr. Bascomb call himself a native son of Wickam City?
3. What are the main issues in the campaign, according to Mr. Bascomb?
4. What is the state of the economy in Wickam City?
5. Why does Mr. Bascomb want to build a toy factory in City Park?
6. What are Mr. Jackson's feelings about the toy factory?
7. What will happen if the toy company doesn't get permission to use City Park?
8. What will happen if there is no new business in Wickam City?
9. Do you think it's more important to build new factories or to protect the environment?
10. Who do you think should be the next mayor of Wickam City: Mr. Jackson or Mr. Bascomb?

PRACTICE • *Add question tags to the following sentences.*

> Mr. Bascomb has been making a lot of speeches.
> **Mr. Bascomb has been making a lot of speeches, hasn't he?**
>
> You aren't voting for him.
> **You aren't voting for him, are you?**

1. He was on TV yesterday.
2. You didn't see him.
3. You haven't talked to him.
4. He's a very busy man.
5. He doesn't have much free time.
6. He wants to build a factory in City Park.
7. The park isn't a good place for a factory.
8. Most people disagree with Mr. Bascomb.
9. He won't succeed.

WRITTEN EXERCISE • *Complete the sentences.*

> If Mr. Bascomb becomes mayor, *he'll bring more business to Wickam City.*
>
> If the weather is good, *we'll go to the beach.*

1. If Mr. Jackson becomes mayor, _____
2. If I become mayor, _____
3. If it rains tomorrow, _____
4. If we stay home, _____
5. If I have time, _____
6. If Peter gets married, _____
7. If you work hard, _____
8. If you're nice to people, _____

WRITTEN EXERCISE 1 • *Complete the sentences using the words **who, what, when, where, whose,** and **why.***

I wonder _who_ that man was.   Do you know _why_ he ran across the street?

1. We have a friend _whose_ parents live in a beautiful house by the beach.
2. You can understand _why_ they spend a lot of time there.
3. Fred is worried because he doesn't know _what_ to do with his life.
4. He'll certainly feel better _when_ he finds a job.
5. The girl _whose_ team lost the basketball game was very unhappy.
6. She left in a hurry and didn't tell anyone _when_ she went.
7. I had my keys _when_ I left the house this morning, but now I can't find them.
8. I wonder _where_ I put my keys.

WRITTEN EXERCISE 2 • *Find the mistake in each sentence and rewrite the sentence correctly.*

The man has a big dog who lives in that house.

The man who lives in that house has a big dog.

I have a friend her father is an opera singer.

I have a friend whose father is an opera singer.

1. That's the market we used to shop at.

    _____

2. The dinner was delicious that your mother made.

    _____

3. Do you know who belongs to this radio?

    _____

4. I met the woman you were talking about her son.

    _____

5. I'd like to find out where do they live.

    _____

6. Could you tell me what time is it?

    _____

7. Let's find a place we can have a quiet conversation there.

    _____

8. Do you know is there a coffee shop nearby?

    _____

GROUP WORK 2 • *What kind of things upset you? Discuss your "gripes" and share them with the class.*

Review • Chapter 2   **35**

There are many different kinds of weddings in the United States, reflecting the different religious and ethnic backgrounds of the American people. Weddings may be large or small, religious or civil, formal or informal—it all depends on the wishes and personal situations of the man and woman who are getting married. An overwhelming majority of today's couples, however, choose to marry in a traditional religious ceremony.

The Wedding Ceremony. There are several customs Americans follow when a man and a woman have a traditional wedding. One of the oldest customs is for the bride to wear "something old, something new, something borrowed, something blue." When the bride enters the church or synagogue, everyone stands up. The processional music starts and the bride walks down the aisle, accompanied by her father. At the end of the aisle, she meets the groom and the officiant (priest, minister, or rabbi) who makes some introductory remarks on marriage. He asks if the couple marries freely, and they answer affirmatively. The bride and groom join hands and declare their vows. After they say their "I do's," the bride and groom exchange rings and they kiss. Then the officiant gives the couple his blessings—they are now officially married. The bride and groom come back down the aisle,

followed by their attendants and families. This completes the ceremony. Outside the church or synagogue, the guests rush up to congratulate the couple and wish them well.

The Wedding Reception. After the wedding ceremony, there is usually a reception at a hotel, restaurant , or private club. The wedding reception is a festive celebration that gives family and friends an opportunity to share the joy of the bride and groom. As with any other special occasion, there is food, drink, and music to make everyone relaxed and happy.

Dancing. If there is dancing at the wedding party, the first dance is reserved for the bride and groom. The music for this formal dance is soft and romantic. After the bride dances with her new husband, the rest of the bridal party joins in and the guests may follow. At this point, the musicians can pick up the tempo and play anything from rock to country to salsa.

Cutting the Cake. One of the wedding's most precious and memorable moments is the cutting of the wedding cake. The bride and groom together make the first cut and they offer each other a piece of cake. This act of sharing symbolizes their lifetime of sharing ahead.

Tossing the Bouquet. At the end of the celebration, all the unmarried women gather for the tossing of the bouquet. Traditionally, the bride turns her back to the women and tosses the bouquet over her shoulder. Today she may face them. Supposedly, the one who catches it will be the next to get married.

Taking Leave. After the bouquet is thrown, the bride and groom leave the reception to begin their honeymoon. The guests wave good-bye to the couple as they leave the party. They drive off in the groom's car, which is often decorated with streamers and flowers.

Modern couples may or may not choose to follow the traditional customs mentioned above, but there is one thing they all have in common: they want their marriage to be successful and their wedding to be as lovely and memorable as they can make it.

1. Why are there many different kinds of weddings in the United States?
2. Do most of today's couples marry in religious ceremonies or civil ceremonies?
3. What happens when the bride enters the church?
4. Who waits for the bride at the end of the aisle?
5. What happens after the bride and groom exchange rings?
6. What happens after the wedding ceremony is over?
7. What do people do at a wedding reception?
8. Who does the bride dance with first? What happens after that?
9. Who makes the first cut in the wedding cake?
10. What is supposed to happen to the woman who catches the bridal bouquet?
11. Where does the couple go after the wedding?

FREE RESPONSE

1. When was the last time you went to a wedding? What was it like?
2. Describe some wedding customs in your country and compare them to wedding customs in the United States.
3. Who usually pays for the wedding in your country?
4. What kind of gifts do people give to the bride and groom in your country?
5. Do you enjoy going to weddings? Why or why not?

TALKING ABOUT CHILDREN

Marty and Jenny are ten years old. They are in the same class and often play together after school.

1. When was the last time you observed children at play?
2. What funny, silly, or unusual things do they do?
3. How did you have fun when you were a child? What games did you play?
4. Do you think today's children grow up too fast?
5. What can we learn from children?

GROUP WORK • *Discuss your childhood. Ask other students about the things they used to do with their family and friends when they were young.*

TALKING ABOUT MARRIAGE

Peter and Tino have been friends for a long time. When Tino got married a few months ago, Peter came to the wedding. Although Peter has a lot of friends who are happily married, he himself would rather be a bachelor.

1. What is your opinion of marriage?
2. What are the advantages of being married?
3. What are the advantages of being single?
4. How does marriage change people?
5. What are some things a husband and wife should do in order to have a happy marriage?

ROLE PLAY 1

Student A plays the part of Peter. Student B plays Tino.

Situation: Tino tries to convince Peter that he would be happier if he had a wife. He points out the advantages of being married. Peter tells Tino that he enjoys his life as a bachelor. He points out the advantages of being single.

ROLE PLAY 2

Student A plays the part of Tino. Student B plays Barbara.

Situation: It's Saturday night. Barbara and Tino are trying to decide whether to go dancing or to a movie. Barbara says they should go dancing because they haven't gone in a long time and they need the exercise. She says there's a good band playing at the Rainbow Club. Tino says it's too expensive to go dancing, and the loud music always gives him a headache. He says there's a good movie at the Rex Cinema, and it only costs a couple of dollars.

COMPOSITION

1. Write about children. What can we learn from them? What are some qualities children lose when they become adults?
2. What are your feelings about marriage? What are the advantages of marriage? What do you think is necessary for a happy marriage?

VOCABULARY

action
activity
audience

bachelor
become

confident (adj.)
cost (n.)

depend

elect

fall (v.)
favor (v.)
follower
freedom

graduate (v.)
gripe (n.)

how (conj.)

luck (n.)

mail (v.)
main (adj.)

manage
microphone
motion (v.)

native (adj.)

opinion
opponent

pastime
peace
permission
protect (v.)

quiet (n.)

realistic
realize
relaxed (adj.)
remain (v.)
role

shop (v.)
sincere
sporting goods
stage (n.)
succeed (v.)
suitable

test (n.)
traveler

unemployment
unless

wonder (v.)

EXPRESSIONS

This can't go on.
Time is running out.
We have to take action.

that way
at that point
a great deal of
a couple of

I don't care
You never know.
Anything is possible.

in order to
according to
for your information

I'll bet . . .
It depends . . .
I wonder why . . .

to do without
to grow up
to point out

Go ahead.
I was born here.

FIRST CONDITIONAL

	Present Tense	Future Tense
If	it rains, she studies, you don't try,	we'll stay home she'll pass the test. you won't succeed.

Future Tense		Present Tense
We'll stay home She'll pass the test You won't succeed	if	it rains. she studies. you don't try.

DEFINING RELATIVE CLAUSES
WHOSE

I know a man That's the woman The boy	whose	wife is an actress house is for sale. team won the basketball game is very happy.

WHERE

The restaurant That's the store Do you know a place	where	he works is very expensive. you lost your umbrella. we can have lunch?

QUESTIONS   NOUN CLAUSES

Where did she go?	I wonder	where she went.
When does the bank open?	Can you tell me	when the bank opens?
Why do they work so hard?	She doesn't understand	why they work so hard.
What did he say?	Do you remember	what he said?
Who's coming to the party?	We don't know	who's coming to the party.

NOUN CLAUSES with the verb BE

He was sick yesterday.	That's why he didn't go to work.
She knew the owner of the company.	That's how she got the job.
They're going to City Park.	That's where they play tennis.
We have to get there before five o'clock.	That's when the post office closes.
He's going to buy a new car.	That's what he told me.

Chapter 3

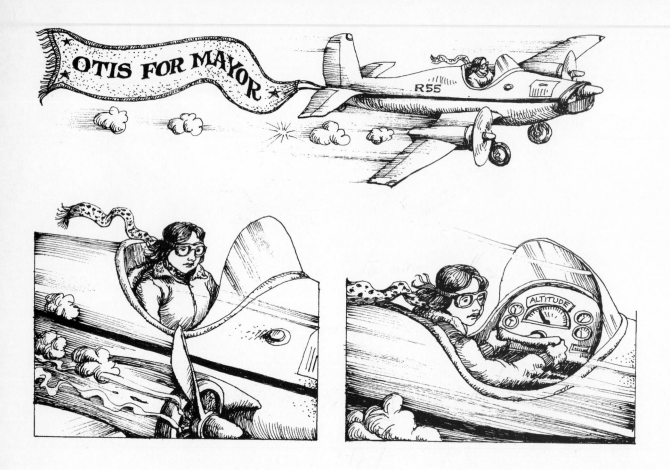

 1. Talk about the pictures.
2. Listen to the story.
3. Answer the story questions.

READING

Nancy Paine has been a pilot for many years. She is an old friend of Otis Jackson's and is supporting his election campaign. Yesterday, Nancy was flying her twin-engine plane over Wickam City with a sign saying OTIS FOR MAYOR. Around two o'clock it started getting cloudy, and Nancy decided to go back to the airport. Suddenly, her right engine began to sputter. It died in less than a minute. Nancy became frightened when the plane started losing altitude. She flew into some heavy clouds and was able to see only a short distance ahead of her. When the clouds disappeared, her plane was just a few hundred feet above the ground. Nancy saw a wheat field in the distance and tried to land there. Unfortunately, her plane was going too fast and she wasn't able to land where she wanted to. She crashed into a barn on the other side of the field. The barn belonged to Elmer Coggins, who was feeding his chickens when he heard the noise. Elmer ran over to the barn and found Nancy inside the plane. She had a concussion and a broken leg, and she wasn't able to move. Although she was badly hurt, Nancy was able to explain what happened. She was in great pain, and after a few minutes she lost consciousness. Elmer opened the door of the plane and gently pulled her out. He laid Nancy on a pile of hay and tried to make her comfortable. Then he ran to the farmhouse and called an ambulance.

1. Why was Nancy flying over Wickam City yesterday?
2. What happened as she was going back to the airport?
3. Was Nancy frightened?
4. Where did she try to make a landing?
5. Why wasn't she able to land in the field?
6. Did she crash into a barn or a farmhouse?
7. Who did the barn belong to?
8. What was Elmer doing when he heard the crash?
9. Where did he find Nancy?
10. Why wasn't she able to move?
11. What did Elmer do?

WRITTEN EXERCISE • *Complete the sentences using the affirmative or negative form of* **be able to** *in the past.*

Her plane was going so fast she *wasn't able to* land where she wanted to.

Although she was badly hurt, she *was able to* explain what happened.

1. Although he was poor, he ___*was able to*___ go to college.

2. He didn't know anyone at the bank, but he ___*was able to*___ get a loan.

3. We were so busy last week we ___*weren't able to*___ come to your party.

4. Although I had a headache, I ___*was able to*___ do my homework.

5. She had no money, so she ___*wasn't able to*___ buy a present for her mother.

6. Her apartment was so small she ___*wasn't able to*___ invite her friends over for dinner.

7. Although he didn't have much experience, he ___*was able to*___ repair his car.

8. It rained Sunday afternoon, so we ___*weren't able to*___ have a picnic at the park.

Listen and practice.

JOHNNIE: Where were you yesterday afternoon? I was trying to find you.

ANNE: I went to the hospital to see Nancy.

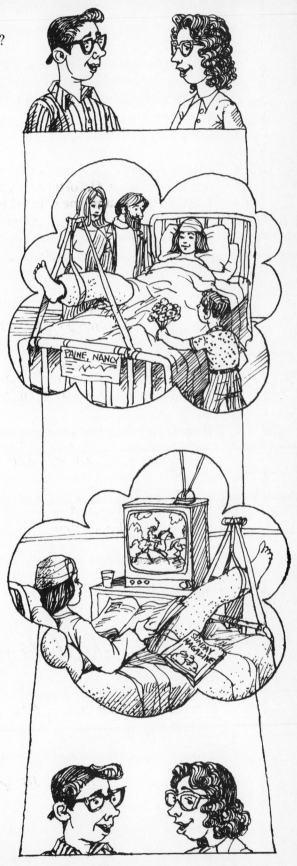

JOHNNIE: How is she doing?

ANNE: Much better. At first she wasn't able to receive any visitors except family members. Now she can see anyone she wants.

JOHNNIE: Can she get out of bed and move around?

ANNE: No, it's still too early. She won't be able to move around until next week.

JOHNNIE: I feel sorry for Nancy. It must be boring to lie in bed all day.

ANNE: It isn't too bad. At least she can sit up and watch television. And she does a lot of reading.

JOHNNIE: How soon will she be able to leave the hospital?

ANNE: I don't know. It depends on how fast she recovers.

JOHNNIE: Do you think she'll ever fly again?

ANNE: Yes. She'll be able to fly in a few months. But she'll need a new airplane. That's for sure.

WRITTEN EXERCISE • *Complete the sentences using* **will be able to.**

Nancy can't leave the hospital yet. She isn't well enough.

The doctor says _she'll be able to leave the hospital_ in a few weeks.

Jimmy can't drive a car yet. He's still too young.

His father says _he'll be able to drive a car_ when he's eighteen.

1. Our baby sister can't walk yet. It's still too early.

   The doctor says _she'll be able to walk_ in a couple of months.

2. Jenny can't wear makeup yet. She isn't old enough.

   Her mother says _she'll be able to wear makeup_ when she's fourteen.

3. She can't go out with boys yet. She's still too young.

   Her mother says _she'll be able to go out with boys_ when she's in high school.

4. Marty can't play on the football team yet. He's too small.

   The coach says _he'll be able to play on the football team_ when he's a little bigger.

5. Barbara can't take her vacation yet. There's too much work.

   Mr. Bascomb says _it'll be able to take her vacation_ in July.

6. Mr. and Mrs. Golo can't buy a new house yet. They haven't saved enough money.

   Mr. Golo says _We'll be able to buy a new house_ next year.

7. Mr. Green can't retire yet. He hasn't worked for the company long enough.

   His boss says _he'll be able to retire_ in three years.

8. Linda can't travel yet. She's still too young.

   Her father says _she'll be able to travel_ when she's a little older.

9. We can't use our washing machine yet. The workman is still repairing it.

   He says _we'll be able to use our washing_ tomorrow.

10. Mr. Bascomb can't make a decision yet. He doesn't have enough information.

    His secretary says _he'll be able to make a decision_ in a few days.

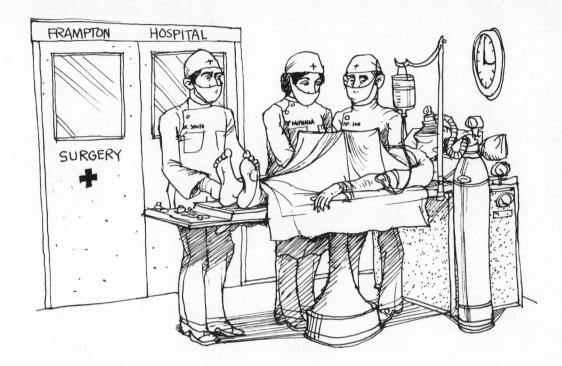

Frampton Hospital is the largest public hospital in Wickam City. It has an excellent staff of doctors and the most modern facilities, including a brand-new X-ray laboratory. Nowadays, the cost of medical care is very high, and Frampton Hospital is no exception. Fortunately, most people in Wickam City have some kind of health insurance that pays at least part of their medical expenses while they are in the hospital.

In the United States, most companies provide health insurance for their employees. However, there are millions of Americans who have no health insurance because they are unemployed and can't afford it, or their companies don't provide it. Uninsured people, most of them poor, don't get regular checkups and often wait until they are quite sick before coming to the hospital. The cost of their treatment is very high, and the state ends up paying for it.

The U.S. health care system pays tremendous additional costs because most Americans don't take good care of their health. They eat too many foods that are high in cholesterol, such as meat and dairy products, and not enough fresh fruit and vegetables. Moreover, Americans have too much stress in their lives, and they don't get enough exercise. Americans would live longer and save billions of dollars in medical expenses by taking better care of their health.

At Frampton Hospital, the doctors try to help their patients by giving them advice on exercise and nutrition. One of the most popular doctors is Maria Miranda. She is very kind to her patients and gives them a lot of attention. One of her newest patients is Nancy Paine, who was injured in a plane crash last week. Nancy was glad that Maria was able to take care of her since they are good friends, and Nancy knows that Maria is an excellent doctor.

Last Sunday Nancy had a lot of visitors, and they brought her some nice presents. At the end of the day Maria came by and the two women had a pleasant talk.

"How are you feeling today?" asked Maria, as she entered the room.

"Much better," said Nancy. "A lot of people came to see me this weekend, and look at all the nice things they brought."

"Those flowers are beautiful," said Maria, "Hmm. They smell good."

"Barney brought them. He was here this morning."

"I understand he's going to be in the movies," said Maria. "Did he tell you?"

"Yes, he told me all about it. He's going to play the part of a taxi driver, which should be easy for him." Nancy smiled as she thought about Barney and the way he described his meeting with Ula Hackey.

"Those pictures look interesting," said Maria, pointing to some photographs on the table. "May I see them?"

"Of course," said Nancy. She picked up the photographs and handed them to Maria. "Aren't they beautiful? Dr. Pasto gave them to me."

"That's nice," said Maria. "Who else came to see you this weekend?"

"Well, Anne was here yesterday. She brought me a box of chocolates. And Otis came by a little while ago with some magazines and a book."

"That was a good idea," said Maria. "You might as well take advantage of this opportunity and do some reading."

"You're right," said Nancy. "My only regret is that I may not be able to help Otis any more with his campaign for mayor. It means so much to me."

"You won't be able to fly your plane again for quite a while, if that's what you mean. But I'm sure there are other ways you can help Otis."

"You're probably right," said Nancy. But there's something else that worries me. My insurance only covers the first week I'm in the hospital, and I've already been here for five days. Do you think I might be able to stay with my family next week?"

"It's up to you," said Maria. "But please talk to me again before you do anything."

"You can count on it," said Nancy.

"That's good. Is there anything special I can do for you while you're here?"

"There is one thing," said Nancy. "I hate to complain, but the food in this hospital tastes awful."

"I'll see what I can do about it," said Maria. "I'm sure we can work something out. Let's see, maybe Tino can bring you some food from the restaurant. I'll ask him."

"Oh Maria, you're so wonderful. No wonder all the patients like you."

"Take it easy with the compliments. They'll go to my head! Well, I've got to go now. I promised to call Peter. See you later, Nancy."

"Goodbye, Maria. Thanks for everything."

STORY QUESTIONS

1. What can you say about the cost of medical care nowadays?
2. What does health insurance do for people?
3. Why are there so many people in the United States without health insurance?
4. Why don't poor people get regular checkups?
5. Who pays for their treatment when they get sick?
6. What do many Americans do that is bad for their health?
7. How do the doctors at Frampton Hospital try to help their patients?
8. Why is Maria Miranda popular with her patients?
9. How long has Nancy Paine been a patient at the hospital?
10. What did Nancy's friends bring her?
11. What is Nancy's only regret?
12. Will she be able to fly again soon?
13. Why is she worried about her insurance?
14. What does the hospital food taste like, according to Nancy?
15. Is there anything Maria can do about it?

TALKING ABOUT HEALTH CARE

1. Have you ever been in the hospital? When? What happened?
2. Do you have health insurance? What kind?
3. Who do you think should pay for each person's health care: the individual, the company he or she works for, or the government?
4. When the government pays, where does the money come from?
5. Does your country have a good health care system?
6. Have you ever been sick for a long time? Who took care of you?
7. How often do you see your doctor?
8. What can you do to stay healthy?

PAIR WORK 1 • *Find out if your partner has ever had an injury. Ask questions to get the details. Then tell the class about your partner's injury.*

"Nancy broke her leg last week. She was flying her plane when the engine died and she crashed into a barn. She was in the hospital for five days."

PAIR WORK 2 • *Have conversations similar to the examples.*

A: Mrs. Golo wants to learn how to dance.
B: **If she takes lessons, she'll be able to dance in a few months.**

A: Dr. Pasto wants to learn how to cook Chinese food.
B: **If he takes lessons, he'll be able to cook Chinese food in a few weeks.**

1. Linda wants to learn how to sew.
2. Fred wants to learn how to dance.
3. Jenny wants to learn how to swim.
4. Albert wants to learn how to ski.
5. Peter wants to learn how to play tennis.
6. Anne wants to learn how to drive a car.
7. Johnnie wants to learn how to speak Spanish.
8. Maria wants to learn how to play the guitar.

PRACTICE • *Complete the sentences using **won't be able to**.*

> Mrs. Hamby loves to eat rich food.
> But if she follows her doctor's advice...
> **she won't be able to eat rich food any more.**

1. Peter loves to go out with beautiful women.
   But if he gets married . . .

2. Mr. and Mrs. Brown love to work in the garden.
   But if they sell their house . . .

3. Otis loves to spend his afternoons in the park.
   But if he becomes mayor . . .

4. Jimmy and Linda love to have noisy parties.
   But if the neighbors complain too much . . .

5. Jenny loves to wear her old jeans.
   But if she keeps growing . . .

6. Fred loves to get up at noon.
   But if he takes a job at the post office . . .

7. We love to play tennis.
   But if they close the park . . .

8. Mr. Golo loves to work at home.
   But if his wife complains too much . . .

9. He loves to drive a big car.
   But if gasoline becomes too expensive . . .

PAIR WORK • *Take turns asking questions about the future. Answer the questions using these expressions: **I think so, I hope so, I'm afraid so, I don't think so, I hope not,** and **I'm afraid not.***

> A: **Will you get more exercise?**
> B: **I hope so.** OR **I'm afraid not.**

1. Will you be busier?
2. Will you have more homework?
3. Will you know a lot more English?
4. Will you have many new friends?
5. Will you be married?
6. Will you have more problems?
7. Will you move to another city?
8. Will you take a long vacation?
9. Will you study another language?

GROUP WORK • *Think about something you plan to do in the future. Then ask the others about their plans. Get the details by asking information questions. For example, if some people in your group plan to take vacations, ask them when and where, and ask what they plan to do on their vacations.*

In most parts of the world, people need money in order to live. They use money to pay for food, clothes, housing, transportation—everything they need for survival. Although money is important to everyone, different people have different attitudes toward money. How they get it and what they do with it say a lot about what kind of people they are.

History tells us there have always been honest people and dishonest people in the world. Surely, most people are honest and work hard for their money. But there are others, the dishonest ones, who have enriched themselves by breaking the law. In the news we often hear about the criminal activities of robbers, drug dealers, and corrupt officials. And we hear about con artists who make large sums of money selling worthless goods, such as fake jewelry and miracle cures that don't work. Con artists know from experience that it's easy to separate fools from their money, and they are always finding new ways to do it. Since most crimes involve money, we can understand why people say "love of money is the root of all evil." We also hear that "crime doesn't pay," since most criminals eventually end up in prison.

Listening to the news, it's easy to get the impression that the world is overrun with dishonest people. But for every dishonest person, there are many more who are honest They know that "money isn't everything" and that honesty has its own rewards. A good example is Abraham Lincoln. When he was a young man, Lincoln had a job working in a general store. One day he mistakenly overcharged one of his customers. When he realized his mistake, Lincoln walked several miles to the man's house to give him the correct change. The man was surprised and delighted, and he told everyone about Lincoln's honesty. It was because of deeds like this that Lincoln became known as "Honest Abe." Lincoln came from a poor family, but his parents taught him the importance of being honest, and the lesson served him well. Years later, Lincoln's reputation for honesty helped him in his political career, and it was one of the reasons he got elected president of the United States. People who will do anything to get money forget that their reputations are worth more than money.

How people get their money is one thing; what they do with it is something else. Some people love to spend money and "live it up." They want to enjoy themselves today and not worry about tomorrow. They are often very generous and like to buy expensive presents for their friends. These people are known as big spenders. At the opposite extreme are the penny pinchers, people who try to save as much as they can for "a rainy day." They often say things like "money doesn't grow on trees" and "a penny saved is a penny earned." They have a reputation for being "cheap" because they are always looking for bargains and hardly ever spend money on other people. When they go to a restaurant, for example, they often let someone else pay the bill. "Cheapskates" aren't very popular because they put money before friendship.

Big spenders and cheapskates both make mistakes when it comes to money and friendship. Big spenders often make the mistake of trying to buy friendship with money. They forget that true friends like you for who you are and not for your money. On the other hand, cheapskates are wrong in thinking that only money can save them in an emergency, that "nobody knows you when you're down and out." They forget that true friends will stand by you even when you are broke. True friendship doesn't depend on money, and, like an honest reputation, friendship has its own rewards. People may need money in order to survive, but they need friends in order to be happy.

1. Why is money important?
2. How do honest people get their money?
3. How do con artists make money?
4. Why do people say "love of money is the root of all evil"? Do you agree?
5. Who was Abraham Lincoln? How did he get the name "Honest Abe"?
6. Describe a big spender. Describe a cheapskate.
7. Do big spenders have more fun than cheapskates? Why or why not?
8. Explain the saying "money doesn't grow on trees."
9. Explain the saying "nobody knows you when you're down and out." Do you think it's true?

FREE RESPONSE

1. Do you think there are more honest people or dishonest people in the world?
2. Do you think a person's reputation is worth more than money? Why?
3. Do you think it's possible to buy friendship with money?
4. Which would you rather have: a lot of friends, or a lot of money?
5. What are some things money can't buy?
6. What's your attitude toward money? Are you a big spender or a cheapskate?

TEST • *Circle the letter next to the most appropriate response.*

1. A cheapskate
   A. loves to spend money.
   B. hates to spend money.
   C. has no money.
   D. uses play money.

2. The opposite of a cheapskate is a
   A. con artist.
   B. politician.
   C. big spender.
   D. penny pincher.

3. Cheapskates are unpopular because
   A. they try to buy friendships.
   B. they are always looking for bargains.
   C. they are always asking for money.
   D. they put money before friendship.

4. Big spenders often
   A. hide their money.
   B. buy expensive presents.
   C. refuse to pay their bills.
   D. take the bus to work.

5. Big spenders say things like
   A. "love of money is the root of all evil."
   B. "let's live it up."
   C. "the best things in life are free."
   D. "a penny saved is a penny earned."

6. Con artists know that
   A. their reputations are worth more than money.
   B. it's easy to separate fools from their money.
   C. money can make you rich.
   D. money isn't everything.

7. Most criminals eventually
   A. become politicians.
   B. take long vacations.
   C. go to prison.
   D. run for president.

8. Abraham Lincoln had a reputation for
   A. honesty.
   B. dishonesty.
   C. overcharging his customers.
   D. taking long walks.

9. Honest people
   A. are never late for work.
   B. work for their money.
   C. don't like to borrow money.
   D. never think about money.

10. Money is important because
    A. it looks good.
    B. you can't buy anything without it.
    C. some people have more than others.
    D. it doesn't grow on trees.

FREE RESPONSE

1. What do you enjoy spending money on?
2. What do you think is a waste of money?
3. Do you spend more money than you make?
4. What can you do to save money?
5. What would you like to have that you can't afford?
6. Do you think rich people are happier than other people?
7. Who is the richest person you can think of? How did this person get rich?
8. Do you think it's easier for dishonest people to get rich?
9. Do you think people who were born poor have a chance to become rich?
10. Do you think anyone can be successful if they work hard?
11. Do you agree that people who work the hardest make the most money?
12. Do you think professional athletes should make more money than teachers? Why?
13. Can a person be successful without making a lot of money?
14. What is your idea of success?
15. What is your idea of a happy life?

TALKING ABOUT SPORTS

Tino is a big sports fan. He enjoys going to football, baseball, and basketball games. He also likes to swim and play tennis.

1. Are you a sports fan? Do you often talk about sports with your friends?
2. What is the most popular sport in your country?
3. What is your favorite team? Who is your favorite player?
4. What sports do you play? Who do you play with? When? Where?
5. Do you prefer group sports or individual sports?
6. What are some benefits of playing a sport?

GROUP WORK • *Talk about sports. What are your favorite teams and players? What sports do you like to play?*

TALKING ABOUT FRIENDSHIP

Nancy has been receiving a lot of visitors at the hospital. She is lucky to have so many good friends.

1. How do you know when you have a friend?
2. Do you find it easy or difficult to make friends?
3. Why is it hard for some people to make friends?
4. What qualities do you look for in a friend?
5. Are most of your friends in the same age group?
6. How did you meet your closest friends?
7. Why do you need friends?

GROUP WORK • *Discuss the most important qualities that you want in a friend. Explain why these qualities are important to you. Choose from the adjectives below or use other adjectives of your own.*

attractive	generous	outgoing	smart
easygoing	honest	patient	understanding
funny	loyal	reliable	warm

TALKING ABOUT HEALTH CARE

1. What is your opinion of the health care system in your country? Is it doing a good job?
2. What are the main problems in your country's health care system? Can you think of some solutions?

COMPOSITION

1. Write about health care in your country. What kind of experiences have you had with hospitals, doctors, and nurses? What can you suggest to make things better?
2. Write about friendship. What makes a good friend?

VOCABULARY

altitude	die (v.)	idiot (n.)	noisy	talk (n.)
around (adv.)		injured		
attention	exception	inside (prep.)	operation	until (prep.)
awful	expense	insurance		
			patient (n.)	voice (n.)
baby (adj.)	facility	laboratory	perfume	
broken	field (n.)	leg (n.)	pull (v.)	washing machine
	fly (v.)	lie (v.)		wheat field
checkup (n.)	fresh (adj.)		regret (n.)	whenever
cotton		margarine		wool
count (v.)	gently	may	special	workman
cover (v.)	ground (n.)	medical	staff (n.)	
crash (n.)		might	suggestion	X-ray (adj.)
crash (v.)	hurt (adj.)			

EXPRESSIONS

I feel sorry for her.
We can work something out.

I'll see what I can do about it.
The state ends up paying for it.

You can count on it.
That's for sure.

Take it easy with the compliments.
They'll go to my head.

Make up your mind.
You have a right to your opinion.

You might as well take advantage of this opportunity.
No wonder all the patients like you.

He came by a little while ago.
I've got to go now.

It's still too early.
It isn't too bad.

It means so much to me.
I wouldn't miss it for anything.

It depends on the weather.
You sound as if you don't care.

to be made of
to be interested in

Say.
Hey!

PAST TENSE with BE ABLE
Affirmative

She	was able	to come.
You	were able	to help.

Negative

She	wasn't able	to come.
You	weren't able	to help.

Interrogative

Was	she	able	to come?
Were	you		to help?

Short Answers

Yes,	she / I	was.

No,	she / I	wasn't.

FUTURE TENSE
Affirmative

He	will be able	to come.
We		to help.

Negative

He	won't be able	to come.
We		to help.

Interrogative

Will	he	be able	to come?
	we		to help?

Short Answers

Yes,	he / we	will.

No,	he / we	won't.

MAY/MIGHT

It	may	rain tomorrow or it	may	be sunny.
She		clean the house or she		watch television.
We	might	stay (at) home or we	might	go to the football game.

VERBS OF PERCEPTION

It	looks feels sounds tastes smells	great. good. OK. bad. terrible.	He It She It It	looks feels sounds tastes smells	like	a basketball player. a summer day. a New Yorker. Swiss chocolate. expensive perfume.

They You	look sound	as if like	they're tired. you're an expert.

Chapter

4

TOPICS
Dating
Finding a job
Meeting people
Politics

GRAMMAR
Review

FUNCTIONS
Making comparisons
Starting a conversation
Inviting someone out
Giving opinions
Making suggestions
Expressing intention

Last Friday Mr. Bascomb decided to take the afternoon off so he could get a haircut. He was walking down Main Street, in the direction of the barber shop, when a dirty, little man approached him. He asked Mr. Bascomb for some money to get something to eat. "I've come all the way from Denver," said the man. "And I haven't had any food for twenty-four hours."

Mr. Bascomb drew back as though the man had a serious disease and handed him a dollar without waiting to receive the man's thanks.

"Poor fellow," said Mr. Bascomb. "Imagine not eating for a whole day." Mr. Bascomb could not imagine this even though he tried, and the idea of going without food seemed such an impossible one that he decided to go back and find the man and give him more money.

Mr. Bascomb's ideas about eating were rather special. He did not know that there were restaurants where one could get a meal for a few dollars, including meat, potatoes, and vegetables. He hardly considered a few dollars a sufficient tip for the waiter who served him his dinner, and certainly not for the dinner itself.

Mr. Bascomb did not see the man at first, and when he finally found him, the man did not see him. Mr. Bascomb stood for a minute watching the man. While he watched him, he saw him stop three other gentlemen, each of whom gave him some money. Then the man approached Mr. Bascomb, repeated his sad story, and asked him for money again. He evidently did not recognize Mr. Bascomb, who gave him two dollars and walked away. He felt the man must certainly have enough money by this time to get something to eat.

An hour later, as Mr. Bascomb was leaving the barber shop, the same man approached him again and gave him the same familiar story. He had just come from Denver, he had not eaten in twenty-four hours, and so on.

This time the man looked a little uneasy. He was not sure whether he had approached this particular gentleman before. But Mr. Bascomb had a clever idea and put his hand quickly into his pocket as if he were about to give the man some money.

"Nothing to eat for twenty-four hours!" said Mr. Bascomb. "And you don't have any money either?"

"Not a cent," said the man sadly, "And I'm weak from lack of food. I hate to ask for money, it's not the money I want. It's just the food. I'm dying from hunger."

"Well," said Mr. Bascomb, "if it's only something to eat that you want, come in here with me and I will buy you lunch." But the man held back and insisted that they would not permit someone like him to enter such a fine restaurant.

"Oh, yes, they will," said Mr. Bascomb, looking at the menu in the window. "It seems to me to be extremely cheap. Go on in!" he added, and there was something in his tone of voice which made the man enter quickly.

The people in the restaurant looked curiously at Mr. Bascomb's elegant dress, his manners, and the carnation in his lapel. They also looked curiously at the miserably dressed person who accompanied him.

"You aren't going to eat two lunches, are you?" asked one of the waiters, addressing himself to Mr. Bascomb's companion. He looked a little uneasy, and Mr. Bascomb, in turn, smiled quietly in triumph.

"You are mistaken," Mr. Bascomb said to the waiter. "This man is starving. He hasn't tasted food for twenty-four hours. Give him whatever he asks for."

Mr. Bascomb's companion looked very unhappy. The waiter smiled and winked at Mr. Bascomb. The man ordered milk, but Mr. Bascomb protested and ordered two steaks, french fries, corn, hot rolls, coffee, and apple pie.

"Heavens! What do you think I am?" cried the man.

"Hungry," said Mr. Bascomb, very softly. "Or are you an impostor? And if you are an impostor, I'll turn you over to the police."

Mr. Bascomb now seemed to be enjoying himself very much. There was a police officer standing across the street, and occasionally Mr. Bascomb would look at his companion and

point toward the police officer. The little man began to eat the food on his plate, but he didn't enjoy it at all. He kept cursing loudly as he ate.

Whenever the man stopped eating, Mr. Bascomb would point to a still unfinished dish, and the man, after strong protest, would attack it again as if it were poison. The people who were sitting nearby were laughing, and the proprietor behind the desk was smiling.

"There," said the man at last. "I've eaten all I can eat for a year. You think you are very clever, don't you? But if you want to spend your money so foolishly, that's your business. Only don't let me catch you around these streets at night, that's all."

And the man started to leave, shaking his fist at Mr. Bascomb.

"Wait a minute," said Mr. Bascomb. "You haven't paid them for your lunch."

"Haven't what?" cried the man. "Paid them? How could I pay them? You invited me here to eat. I didn't want any lunch, did I? You'll have to pay for your fun yourself, or they'll throw you out. Don't try to be too clever."

"I gave you three dollars so you could buy lunch. This check calls for eight dollars, and it's very cheap," said Mr. Bascomb, bowing politely toward the proprietor. "Several other men also gave you money for lunch when you told them you were starving. You have the money with you now. So pay what you owe at once, or I'll call the police officer," he said.

The man started to run toward the door, but the waiter ran after him, took hold of him by the neck, and held him.

"Let me go," cried the man. "Let me go and I'll pay you."

Everybody in the restaurant came up now, formed a circle around the group, and watched the man count out eight dollars into the waiter's hand, which left him just one dollar to himself.

"You have forgotten the waiter who served you," said Mr. Bascomb, smiling and pointing at the one dollar bill which remained.

"No," said the man strongly.

"Oh, yes," said Mr. Bascomb. "Do the right thing now or I'll . . ."

Then the man dropped the one dollar bill into the waiter's hand, and Mr. Bascomb, smiling, made his way through the admiring crowd and out into the street.

"I suspect," said Mr. Bascomb later in the day when retelling his adventure to a friend, "that after I left, the fellow tried to get that tip back from the waiter, for I saw him come out of the place very suddenly without touching the pavement and land on his back in the street. That waiter certainly was a powerful fellow."

1. Describe the man who was asking everyone for money.
2. How much money did Mr. Bascomb give the man the first time?
3. Why did Mr. Bascomb go back a second time to give the man more money?
4. What happened the third time the man asked Mr. Bascomb for money? What did Mr. Bascomb offer to do?
5. What excuse did the man give for not wanting to go into the restaurant?
6. What did the man order for lunch?
7. Why did Mr. Bascomb order more food?
8. Why did the man run toward the door after he had finished his lunch?
9. Who finally paid for the meal?
10. What happened to the man after Mr. Bascomb left the restaurant?
11. What kind of man is Mr. Bascomb? Do you admire him?
12. Have you ever had a stranger ask you for money? What was your reaction?

WRITTEN EXERCISE • *Complete the sentences using **so** and **neither**.*

Tino reads the Wickam Daily News. ___*So does*___ Barbara.

They haven't gone out this week. ___*Neither have*___ I.

1. Johnnie missed the bus. _____ Anne.
2. They're always late. _____ you.
3. We didn't go to the football game. _____ they.
4. She lives on a quiet street. _____ he.
5. He won't get paid this week. _____ she.
6. They've been wasting a lot of time. _____ we.
7. I don't like to get up early. _____ Fred.
8. He isn't very ambitious. _____ Barney.
9. We can do a better job. _____ they.
10. They won't be home Saturday. _____ I.

PAIR WORK • *Ask and answer questions using the present perfect.*

eat Japanese food
A: **Have you ever eaten Japanese food?**
B: **Yes, I have. I ate in a Japanese restaurant last month.**
 OR **No, I haven't. But I've eaten Chinese food.**

1. walk in the rain
2. catch a butterfly
3. climb a mountain
4. sleep under the stars
5. take a cold shower
6. get a bad haircut
7. meet a famous person
8. do something crazy
9. break anything
10. have a car accident
11. lose something valuable
12. help a stranger

PAIR WORK • *Compare the people in the pictures.*

1. A: **Does Ed watch as <u>much</u> television as Johnnie?**
   B: **Yes, he does. He watches <u>more</u> television than Johnnie.**

2. A: **Does Barbara make as <u>many</u> mistakes as Anne?**
   B: **No, she doesn't. Anne makes <u>more</u> mistakes than Barbara.**

3. A: Does Ula Hackey spend as _____ money as Betty?

4. A: Does Jack have as _____ problems as Mr. Farley?

5. A: Does Anne drink as _____ coffee as Johnnie?

6. A: Does Otis eat as _____ vegetables as Gloria?

7. A: Does Jenny read as _____ comic books as Marty?

8. A: Does Fred sleep as _____ as Mr. Bascomb?

Listen and practice.

Dimples is a popular hangout with students. They like to go there and listen to music.

PAIR WORK • *Start a conversation with another student. Use the dialogue between Linda and Joe as a model. Here are some typical opening lines:*

> **Excuse me. Are you waiting for someone?**
> **Haven't I seen you somewhere before?**
> **Do you come here often?**
> **Would you like some company?**

GROUP WORK • *You see someone you don't know but who you would like to meet. It could be anywhere—at school, at work, in a coffee shop, or at a party. Think of some good opening lines you can use to start a conversation. Make a list of the best opening lines and share them with the class.*

DISCUSSION • *When was the last time you met someone by chance? Where and how did it happen? What was the person like? Who spoke first? Do you remember what you said?*

CONVERSATION

Listen and practice.

A few days after meeting Linda, Joe calls her for a date.

JOE: Hi, Linda. It's Joe.

LINDA: Joe! How are you?

JOE: Fine. Are you doing anything Friday night?

LINDA: No. I don't have any plans.

JOE: Well, I was wondering if you'd like to go to a movie.

LINDA: Sure. What would you like to see?

JOE: *Attack of the Ant Men* with Buster Bailey.

LINDA: Oh, I've already seen that one. It wasn't very good.

JOE: Well, we could see *Costume Party*. It's a comedy with Ula Hackey.

LINDA: That sounds good. What time does the show start?

JOE: Eight o'clock. I'll pick you up at seven.

LINDA: Okay. See you Friday night.

PAIR WORK • *Have a similar conversation. Make plans to see a movie with another student. Choose a movie that is playing in your city now.*

Listen and practice.

Joe and Linda are leaving the Rex Theater. They have just seen a comedy called Costume Party.

JOE: What did you think of the movie?

LINDA: It was hilarious—especially the part when Ula Hackey was dancing with the gorilla.

JOE: Yeah, that was pretty wild. She thought it was a man in a gorilla costume, and it turned out to be a real gorilla.

LINDA: What did you think was the best part?

JOE: The food fight. Everybody got into it—even the old ladies.

LINDA: The only thing I didn't like was when the fat man slipped on the banana peel. I felt sorry for him.

JOE: Not me. But I like slapstick.

LINDA: This is the first time I've seen Ula Hackey in a comedy. Wasn't she good?

JOE: She was terrific. I can't wait to see her next movie.

LINDA: Neither can I.

PAIR WORK • *Talk with another student about a movie you have both seen. What did you like about the movie? What parts didn't you like? Did the movie have a good story? Was it realistic, funny, scary, boring? What did you think of the actors?*

TALKING ABOUT DATING

1. At what age do young people start dating in your country?
2. What do they do on a typical date?
3. Do you remember your first date? What was it like?
4. What was the best date or the worst date of your life? Who was it with? What happened?
5. What do you enjoy doing when you go out on a date?
6. Do you have to spend a lot of money to have a good time?
7. What are some good "cheap dates"?

WRITTEN EXERCISE • *Complete the sentences using the words* **so, since, unless, in order to,** *and* **although.**

Our team won the game yesterday _____*although*_____ they played poorly.

Jimmy couldn't throw the ball very well _____*since*_____ he had a sore arm.

You have to practice a lot _____*in order to*_____ be a good player.

1. Sam was tired when he got home, _____ he took a rest.

2. Mabel has stopped eating dessert _____ lose weight.

3. We decided to watch TV _____ we had nothing better to do.

4. You won't be able to finish that job _____ you get some help.

5. Mr. Poole likes sports _____ he isn't a very good athlete.

6. He takes the bus to work _____ save money.

7. His wife doesn't like her job _____ the pay is very good.

8. They will take their vacation next week _____ something happens.

9. Linda wasn't having a good time at the party, _____ she left early.

10. Albert didn't go to the party _____ he wasn't feeling well.

PRACTICE • *Make questions using* **who, what,** *and* **where.**

Anne has been talking to <u>Johnnie</u>.
Who has she been talking to?

They have been meeting <u>in the park</u>.
Where have they been meeting?

They have been saving <u>their old magazines</u>.
What have they been saving?

1. Ed has been spending his afternoons <u>in the library</u>.
2. He has been reading <u>a lot of crime stories</u>.
3. He has been avoiding <u>his old girlfriend</u>.
4. She has been trying to find out <u>what's wrong</u>.
5. She has been going to <u>his favorite hangouts</u>.
6. She has been talking to <u>his friends</u>.
7. They have been telling her <u>things about Ed</u>.
8. She has been trying to see <u>his family</u>.
9. They have been staying <u>at the Regal Hotel</u>.

PAIR WORK • *Take turns asking questions using the present perfect continuous.*

> eating a lot of sweets
> A: **Have you been eating a lot of sweets?**
> B: **Yes, I have. I've been eating too much candy lately.**
>   OR **No, I haven't. I try to avoid eating sweets.**
>   OR **No. I don't like sweets.**

1. going out a lot
2. meeting a lot of people
3. spending a lot of money
4. working hard

5. getting a lot of exercise
6. watching TV a lot
7. going to bed late
8. getting enough sleep

PRACTICE • *Make sentences using **who, whose,** or **where.***

> He didn't talk to Jane. He talked to someone else.
> **I wonder <u>who</u> he talked to.**
>
> She didn't go to work. She went somewhere else.
> **I wonder <u>where</u> she went.**
>
> They didn't use our computer. They used someone else's computer.
> **I wonder <u>whose</u> computer they used.**

1. Peter didn't borrow Maria's camera. He borrowed someone else's camera.
2. He didn't give me the photographs. He gave them to someone else.
3. Maria didn't go to the park. She went somewhere else.
4. She didn't drive her own car. She drove someone else's car.
5. Barney didn't call his girlfriend. He called someone else.
6. They didn't have dinner at Joe's Cafe. They had dinner somewhere else.
7. They didn't go to Gloria's party. They went to someone else's party.
8. Linda didn't make a date with Albert. She made a date with someone else.
9. They didn't study at the library. They studied somewhere else.

WRITTEN EXERCISE • *Write sentences about yourself that begin with these expressions:*

> I can't remember _____ *where I left my keys.* _____
> I'm not sure _____ *if I paid the phone bill.* _____

1. I wonder _____

2. I don't know _____

3. I'm not sure _____

4. I'd like to find out _____

5. I don't understand _____

6. I can't remember _____

WRITTEN EXERCISE • *Complete the sentences using the words **who, what, where, when, whose,** and **why.***

I wonder _when_ the party starts.

Do you know _who_ is coming to the party?

1. The boy _____ team lost the football game was very unhappy.

2. He talked so fast I couldn't understand _____ he was saying.

3. The woman _____ lives in that house has a lot of valuable paintings.

4. I don't know _____ she never told you about her paintings.

5. This pen isn't mine. I wonder _____ pen it is.

6. Please close the door _____ you leave the room.

7. Did you hear about _____ happened last night?

8. Someone robbed the store _____ my sister works.

9. She saw the man _____ took the money.

10. She was afraid. That's _____ she didn't call the police.

11. The robber turned off the lights _____ he left the store.

12. Nobody knows _____ he went.

PAIR WORK • *Student A makes a statement. Student B expresses disagreement by using a short sentence.*

A: **Dogs are smarter than cats.**   B: **No, they aren't.**
A: **Money can't buy happiness.**   B: **Yes, it can.**
A: **Ms. Benton drives a Cadillac.**   B: **No, she doesn't.**

1. A: The Golos sold their house last week.   B: _____

2. A: They're going to live in Canada.   B: _____

3. A: The bank was closed yesterday.   B: _____

4. A: Mr. Bascomb didn't go to work.   B: _____

5. A: He doesn't like his job.   B: _____

6. A: He's very lazy.   B: _____

7. A: Jenny has been watching TV all day.   B: _____

8. A: She hasn't done her homework yet.   B: _____

9. A: She isn't a very good student.   B: _____

10. A: She gets poor grades in school.   B: _____

11. A: We can't see our friends tonight.   B: _____

12. A: We won't have enough time.   B: _____

GROUP WORK 1 • *Suggest steps that a person might take to find a job. Make a list of your suggestions and share them with the class.*

GROUP WORK 2 • *Suggest some things a person can do to meet people and make new friends. Make a list of your suggestions and share them with the class.*

GETTING THE DETAILS

ROLE PLAY 1 • *Student A has just gotten a job. Student B wants to know the details. Ask these questions and others of your own.*

- Where?
- What do you do?
- Is it interesting?
- Does it pay well?
- How did you find it?

ROLE PLAY 2 • *Student A has just had a wonderful date. Student B wants to know the details. Ask these questions and others of your own.*

- Who did you go out with?
- What was he/she like?
- Where did you go?
- What did you do?
- Are you going to see him/her again?

🔊 *Listen and practice.*

A: Vote for me!

B: Why? Give me one good reason.

A: If you elect me, I'll *lower your taxes.*

B: Sounds good. You have my vote.

OR Hmm . . . I'll have to think about it.

OR You must be joking.

OR I don't believe you.

PAIR WORK • *Have similar conversations. Student A is a candidate for mayor. Student B is a voter. The candidate makes promises and the voter responds.*

1. save City Park

2. feed the hungry

3. create new jobs

4. make the streets safe

5. put the criminals in jail

6. improve transportation

7. eliminate pollution

8. build more schools

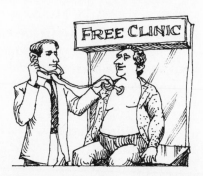

9. provide better health care

TALKING ABOUT POLITICS

1. Have you ever heard a campaign speech? When? Where?
2. Do you think the best candidate usually wins in elections?
3. Why is it important to vote?
4. Who are the most important political leaders in your country?
5. What political leader do you admire most? Least? Why?
6. What are the most important issues in your country today?
7. Are problems such as crime and unemployment getting better or worse?
8. What do you think should be done about crime and unemployment?
9. Would you like to be the leader of your country? Why or why not?

WRITTEN EXERCISE • *Complete the sentences using **someone, something, somewhere, anyone, anything,** and **anywhere.***

Marty has ___*something*___ in his pocket.

Don't tell ___*anyone*___ about our plans.

The umbrella is ___*somewhere*___ in the closet.

1. Come here. There's ___*something*___ I have to tell you.
2. My sister didn't give me ___*anything*___ for my birthday.
3. She's busy now. She's talking to ___*someone*___ on the phone.
4. We stayed home last night. We didn't go ___*anywhere*___.
5. I've never met ___*anyone*___ like Mr. Poole.
6. He can't do ___*anything*___ right.
7. That woman looks familiar. I've seen her ___*someone*___ before.
8. She's lonely. She needs ___*someone*___ to talk to.
9. I've lost my watch! I can't find it ___*anywhere*___.
10. Has ___*anyone*___ seen my gold watch?
11. If you're hungry, we can get ___*something*___ to eat at Joe's Cafe.
12. I don't like Joe's Cafe. Let's go ___*somewhere*___ else.

PAIR WORK • *Take turns asking questions. Answer using **might.***

A: **What are you going to do tonight?**
B: **I don't know. I might see some friends.** OR **I might read a book.**

1. What are you going to do after this class is over?
2. What are you going to do when you get home?
3. What are you going to have for dinner?
4. What are you going to give your mother for her birthday?
5. What are you going to do tomorrow?
6. What are you going to do this weekend?
7. What are you going to buy the next time you go shopping?
8. Where are you going to go on your next vacation?

1. Have you ever been to a costume party? What did you wear?
2. Describe a wonderful party you went to. What made it special?
3. What are your plans for this evening? Tomorrow? This weekend?
4. Do you like to cook? What kinds of dishes can you make?
5. Can you recommend a good restaurant? Why do you think it's good?
6. What's your favorite kind of entertainment?
7. When was the last time you had a good laugh? What was so funny?
8. When was the last time you forgot something? What was it?
9. Have you done anyone a favor recently? Has anyone done you a favor?
10. Do you think it's important to help others? Why?

VOCABULARY

approach	fellow	milk shake	retell
attack (n.)	foolishly	modest	
attack (v.)			slip (v.)
	hangout	neck	strongly
bikini	hilarious		suspect
		occasionally	
costume	impossible		terrific
	insist	particular	
disease		pasta	uneasy
	lack	permit	unfinished
evidently	latter	protest (n.)	
extremely		protest (v.)	whether
	manners		

EXPRESSIONS

I'm dying from hunger.
That's your business.
Do the right thing.
I'll turn you over to the police.
You must be joking.

Heavens!
It has a good beat.
It was pretty wild.
He took the afternoon off.
He made his way through the crowd.

at once
by this time
by the way
tone of voice
to take hold of

I was wondering if you'd like to . . .
Sounds good.

1. Anne doesn't have _____ clothes.
   A. much   C. no
   B. many   D. some

2. I'm not ready. Can you wait
   _____ minutes?
   A. much   C. a few
   B. many   D. a lot of

3. You won't find _____ information in that book.
   A. much   C. no
   B. many   D. some

4. Fred's apartment is almost empty.
   He has very _____ furniture.
   A. much   C. few
   B. many   D. little

5. Where's my dictionary? I can't
   find it _____ .
   A. somewhere   C. nowhere
   B. anywhere   D. everywhere

6. You missed a great party last
   night. _____ was there.
   A. Someone   C. No one
   B. Anyone   D. Everyone

7. I'm hungry. I want _____ to eat.
   A. something   C. nothing
   B. anything   D. everything

8. Ed and Fred are both lazy.
   _____ of them likes to work.
   A. Either   C. One
   B. Neither   D. None

9. The manager _____ our
   apartment building is very friendly.
   A. of   C. from
   B. to   D. with

10. Nancy lives _____ Oak Street.
    A. at   C. in
    B. on   D. to

11. The dog entered the house _____ the back door.
    A. under   C. through
    B. over   D. around

12. Peter wants to take a trip _____ the world.
    A. under   C. through
    B. over   D. around

13. If you want to be successful, you have to
    work _____ .
    A. good   C. hard
    B. quick   D. intelligent

14. Maria is _____ because she can't
    find her keys.
    A. relaxed   C. tired
    B. worried   D. bored

15. It _____ all day. I wonder when it
    will stop.
    A. rains   C. rained
    B. is raining   D. has been raining

16. Sandy isn't home now. She _____
    at the office.
    A. works   C. worked
    B. is working   D. has worked

17. If you _____ more, you
    will feel better.
    A. exercise   C. will exercise
    B. are exercising D. exercised

18. The Browns often _____ steak
    and french fries. It's their favorite dinner.
    A. eat   C. have eaten
    B. are eating   D. were eating

19. Joe and Linda _____ to a party
    last night.
    A. go   C. have gone
    B. went   D. have been

20. Joe _____ here since 1985.
    A. lives   C. lived
    B. is living   D. has been living

21. I _____ of you when you called the other day.
    A. think
    B. am thinking
    C. was thinking
    D. have thought

22. Barney _____ a taxi for many years, and he has never had an accident.
    A. drives
    B. is driving
    C. drove
    D. has driven

23. Hurry up! I'm afraid we _____ be late for the meeting.
    A. will
    B. must
    C. can
    D. should

24. You'd better take your notebook.
    You _____ need it.
    A. must
    B. can
    C. should
    D. might

25. _____ I borrow your pen?
    A. Must
    B. May
    C. Will
    D. Shall

26. Mr. Bascomb works too hard. He _____ relax more.
    A. shall
    B. can
    C. should
    D. would

27. He worked twelve hours today.
    He _____ be tired.
    A. must
    B. will
    C. can
    D. would

28. Jenny doesn't like horror movies.
    I don't like horror movies _____ .
    A. too
    B. also
    C. either
    D. neither

29. She can't go out today _____ she has to study.
    A. but
    B. because
    C. so
    D. although

30. You can come to the party, _____ don't bring your dog.
    A. but
    B. because
    C. so
    D. although

31. We don't have a car, _____ we have to take the bus.
    A. but
    B. because
    C. so
    D. although

32. _____ is the Brown family going?
    To Mom's Cafe.
    A. When
    B. How
    C. Where
    D. Why

33. _____ do they eat out?
    Once a week.
    A. When
    B. How often
    C. Where
    D. Why

34. _____ are they looking at?
    The menu.
    A. Who
    B. Which
    C. Where
    D. What

35. _____ are they eating so fast?
    Because they are in a hurry.
    A. When
    B. What
    C. How
    D. Why

36. _____ waitress is the friendliest?
    Ms. Randolph.
    A. Which
    B. Whose
    C. What
    D. Who

37. I'm _____ tired to walk home.
    A. too
    B. so
    C. very
    D. enough

38. Mona gets up _____ than Fred.
    A. early
    B. more early
    C. earlier
    D. more earlier

39. Fred is the _____ person I've ever known.
    A. lazier
    B. laziest
    C. most lazy
    D. most laziest

40. Tino can lift anything. His _____ is incredible.
    A. size
    B. weight
    C. speed
    D. strength

41. Jimmy has been studying a lot,

    _____ ?

    A. has he   C. hasn't he
    B. he has   D. he hasn't

42. You didn't sell your car, _____ ?

    A. did you   C. didn't you
    B. you did   D. you didn't

43. Do you know the woman _____
    lives across the street?

    A. what   C. which
    B. who   D. there

44. She married a man _____ job is
    selling encyclopedias.

    A. her   C. whose
    B. his   D. which

45. Please _____ the radio. I'm trying
    to study.

    A. put off   C. take off
    B. get off   D. turn off

46. Jenny had the flu last week. It took her

    three days to _____ it.

    A. get over   C. get out of
    B. get away from   D. get through

47. Marty is always talking in class.

    _____ the teacher gets upset.

    A. After all   C. So far
    B. That way   D. No wonder

48. Can you loan me some money?

    A. I'm out of shape.
    B. I'm in a bad mood.
    C. I'm broke.
    D. I'm all right.

Circle the letter that shows where the word in parentheses should be placed in the sentence.

(here)

_____ Mrs. Golo came _____ last week _____ for a visit _____ .
　　A　　　　　　　　　　　　Ⓑ　　　　　　　　　C　　　　　　　D

49. (soon)

    I hope _____ she _____ will come _____ again _____ .
    　　　　　A　　　　　B　　　　　　　　C　　　　　　D

50. (perhaps)

    _____ you _____ can _____ meet her _____ next time.
    　　　A　　　　B　　　　C　　　　　　　　D

Chapter

5

T O P I C S
Military service
Jobs
Leisure activities
Exercise

G R A M M A R
Had to/will have to
Verb + object + infinitive (with "to")
Would rather

F U N C T I O N S
Talking about obligation in the past and future
Interviewing for a job
Expressing preference
Making conclusions
Giving opinions

1. *Talk about the picture.*
2. *Listen to the story.*
3. *Answer the story questions.*

READING

Sam and Jack often talk about their days in the army. It was a hard life. The men had to get up early in the morning and do a lot of physical labor. They had to learn how to use a rifle, and they had to march at least ten miles a day. There wasn't much entertainment; they had to do without television and computer games. The only form of recreation they had was sports. They only made about $80 a month, so they didn't have to worry about where to spend their money. Fortunately, they didn't have to pay any bills since the army paid their expenses. And they didn't have to do their own cooking; the army took care of that, too. In fact, the army took care of everything. The men never had to plan what they were going to do each day since the army did it for them. They had very little freedom in the beginning, but after the first six weeks the situation started to improve. The men didn't have to stay at the base all the time. They could go out on the weekends and see their girlfriends—something Sam and Jack did as often as possible. Jack didn't like being in the army, since he didn't like taking orders. But Sam never complained. He thought being in the army was a good experience, and that everyone should serve their country.

1. What do Sam and Jack often talk about?
2. Did they have to get up early in the morning?
3. How far did they have to march every day?
4. Did they get to watch TV and play computer games?
5. How much money did they make?
6. Why didn't they have to pay any bills?
7. Did the men have much freedom in the beginning?
8. How did the situation improve after the first six weeks?
9. Why didn't Jack like being in the army?
10. Why didn't Sam complain?

PAST OF **HAVE TO** Affirmative

He had to get up early in the morning.

She _____.

You _____.

We _____.

PAIR WORK • *Have conversations similar to the example.*

A: **Jack doesn't like to get up early, does he?**
B: **No, but he had to get up early when he was in the army.**

1. Jack doesn't like to work hard, does he?
2. Jack doesn't like to exercise, does he?
3. Jack doesn't like to shave every day, does he?
4. Jack doesn't like to shine his shoes, does he?
5. Jack doesn't like to make his bed, does he?
6. Jack doesn't like to wear heavy boots, does he?
7. Jack doesn't like to take orders, does he?
8. Jack doesn't like to attend a lot of meetings, does he?
9. Jack doesn't like to hurry, does he?

Listen and practice.

JIMMY: Dad, I want to ask you something.

SAM: Sure. What is it, son?

JIMMY: Do you think I should join the army after I graduate from high school?

SAM: Well, you don't have to join the army, but you should do something for your country.

JIMMY: What'll it be like if I join the army?

SAM: First of all, you'll have to cut your hair. But you won't have to wear it too short.

JIMMY: Will the food be OK?

SAM: Ha! Ha! You'll have to eat a lot of beans, but at least you won't have to do the cooking.

JIMMY: Will I have to carry a rifle?

SAM: Of course, and you'll have to do a lot of marching. But that won't hurt you.

JIMMY: What are the advantages of joining the army?

SAM: You can learn a lot, son. You'll have to work hard, but it's good experience. And when you get out, you'll be ready for college.

JIMMY: That sounds pretty good. I'm going to give it some more thought before I make a decision.

SAM: Sure, Jimmy. Take your time and then decide.

FUTURE OF **HAVE TO** Affirmative

He'll have to work hard.

She'll _____.

You'll _____.

We'll _____.

PAIR WORK • *Have conversations similar to the example.*

A: My brother wants to join the army, but he doesn't like to take orders.

B: **If he wants to join the army, he'll have to take orders.**

1. Albert wants to lose weight, but he doesn't like to exercise.
2. Linda wants to be a good tennis player, but she doesn't like to practice.
3. Anne want to learn Spanish, but she doesn't like to study.
4. Peter wants to go fishing with Tino, but he doesn't like to get up early.
5. My sister wants to go to college, but she doesn't like to study.
6. Jack wants to be a success, but he doesn't like to work hard.
7. Sandy wants to save money, but she doesn't like to eat in cheap restaurants.
8. Barney wants to look good, but he doesn't like to iron his clothes.
9. Mabel wants to please her husband, but she doesn't like to cook Chinese food.
10. Mr. Poole wants to please his wife, but he doesn't like to go to the opera.

FUTURE OF **HAVE TO** Negative

She won't have to go to the store.

He _____.

They _____.

You _____.

PRACTICE • *Make sentences using **won't have to**.*

The dishes are clean. (wash)

You won't have to wash them.

The dog has already eaten. (feed)

You won't have to feed it.

1. The meetings next week aren't very important. (attend)
2. I've already spoken to Mrs. Farley. (call)
3. She knows how to use the computer. (show)
4. Your car is running pretty well. (repair)
5. The garage looks OK. (clean)
6. Sam can lift those boxes. (help)
7. I can go to work with my neighbor. (take)
8. I have an alarm clock. (wake up)
9. The students already know about the music program. (tell)
10. They know how to get to the auditorium. (show)

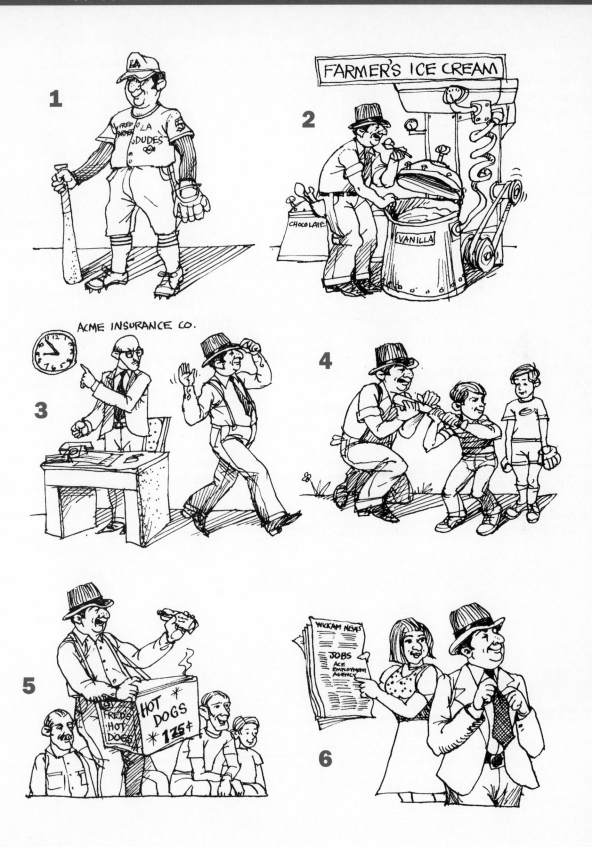

 1. *Talk about the pictures.*
2. *Listen to the story.*
3. *Answer the story questions.*

Fred Farmer has a lot of friends in Wickam City and is very popular with the neighborhood kids. Everyone remembers him as a professional baseball player. Fred used to be with a team in Los Angeles several years ago. He had to give up baseball when he injured his arm in an automobile accident. At the time, everyone expected him to take a job at his father's ice cream factory. But Fred would rather eat ice cream than sell it. Once he tried working for an insurance company downtown. He was supposed to be on the job at 8:30 in the morning, but that was too early for Fred. Besides, he didn't like being in an office all day, so he quit.

Now Fred spends most of his time in the park. He enjoys teaching boys in the neighborhood how to play baseball. Whenever Fred needs a little money, he sells hot dogs at the sports stadium. His sister Mona wants him to get a regular job. Last week she sent him to see a man at the Ace Employment Company. She told Fred to wear a suit and tie for the interview, and she reminded him to be polite. She wanted her brother to make a good impression. Fred seemed to be in good spirits when he went to the employment agency, and Mona was happy, too.

1. What professional sport did Fred used to play?
2. Where did people expect him to work when his baseball career was over?
3. Why wasn't Fred any good at selling ice cream?
4. What other job did he try?
5. Why did he quit working there?
6. Where does Fred spend his time now?
7. Does he teach boys how to play baseball or football?
8. What does Fred do whenever he needs a little money?
9. What does Mona want Fred to do?
10. Where did she send him last week?
11. What did she tell him to wear for the interview?
12. Why did she remind him to be polite?

VERB + OBJECT + INFINITIVE (WITH TO)

She wants him to find a job.

_____ work hard.

_____ be successful.

_____ make a lot of money.

PAIR WORK • *Ask and answer questions.*

A: What did she want him to do—get a job?
B: **That's right. She wanted him to get a job.**

1. What did they expect him to do—work for his father?
2. Where did he invite her to go—to a movie?
3. What did she remind him to take—an umbrella?
4. Who did they want us to meet—Mr. Bascomb?
5. When did he tell us to come—at nine o'clock?
6. Where did she expect him to go—to the store?
7. What did she ask him to buy—some milk?
8. What did they tell us to bring—some hot dogs?

Listen and practice.

MR. GUMBO: Good morning. May I help you?

FRED: Yes, I'm looking for a job.

MR. GUMBO: Well, you've come to the right place. How did you find out about the Ace Employment Company?

FRED: My sister told me to come here.

MR. GUMBO: Very good. First I'm going to ask you to fill out this form.

FRED: I've never seen one of these. Can you show me how to fill it out?

MR. GUMBO: Sure. You're supposed to write your name, address, and telephone number at the top of the page. Then fill in the information about your previous jobs and your education.

FRED: There. I hope you can read my handwriting.

MR. GUMBO: That's fine. Let's see, Fred Farmer . . . Fred Farmer? Aren't you the famous baseball player?

FRED: Well, I used to play some baseball several years ago.

MR. GUMBO: Don't be modest, Fred. You were a great player. I'm sure we can help you. What kind of job are you looking for?

FRED: I want a job that will allow me to work outside. I can't stand being in an office all day.

MR. GUMBO: Would you like to work for the sanitation department? That's an outdoor job.

FRED: Well, I'd rather do something else.

MR. GUMBO:	I'm sorry. That's the only job we have that isn't an office job.
FRED:	I see. Well, thanks anyway, Mr. Gumbo.
MR. GUMBO:	Goodbye, Fred. And good luck.

PAIR WORK • *Have conversations similar to the examples.*

A: **Did Fred know how to fill out the form?**

B: **No. Mr. Gumbo had to show him how to fill out the form.**

A: **Will Gloria be home for lunch?**

B: **I don't think so. We don't expect her to be home for lunch.**

1. **A:** Did Sam go to the market?

   B: I think so. Mabel asked . . .

2. **A:** Will the neighbors bring some food?

   B: I hope so. We reminded . . .

3. **A:** Will Linda clean the kitchen?

   B: Yes. I told . . .

4. **A:** Will Jimmy help her?

   B: He should. We asked . . .

5. **A:** Did Albert pick up the package?

   B: I hope so. We sent . . .

6. **A:** Did Jenny go the party?

   B: Yes. Her mother allowed . . .

7. **A:** Is she learning how to play the piano?

   B: That's right. Ms. Finch is teaching . . .

8. **A:** Will Peter come over tomorrow?

   B: I hope so. We invited . . .

9. **A:** Did he call the hospital?

   B: I think so. Maria asked . . .

10. **A:** Did they find the keys?

    B: Yes. We helped . . .

Wickam City is a wonderful place to live. It has friendly people, sunny weather, and many outstanding tourist attractions. The city is close to the mountains, and it's only a few miles from the Pacific Ocean. There is good skiing in the wintertime, and during the summer months people enjoy camping and fishing at Bear Lake. The Pacific coastline is very beautiful with its golden beaches and redwood forests. The beach season is from June to October. You can play volleyball, swim in the ocean, or just relax and read a good book. There is always a big crowd at the beach on the weekends. People from town like to bring hot dogs and hamburgers and cook them over an open fire. They sing songs, play games, and eat a lot of good food. Everyone has a great time.

Visitors who come to Wickam City always talk about the natural beauty of the surrounding area. They can hardly believe that the mountains and the ocean are so close to the city. With such advantages, you might expect Wickam City to make a lot of money from tourism. However, there isn't much tourist business because the town has only a few first-class hotels. They can't begin to accommodate all the people who would like to stay in Wickam City. It's unfortunate, since the city's economy is in bad shape, and the townspeople could use the extra money that tourism would bring. The current administration has done very little to improve the situation. It's unlikely that anything will happen until after the election when a new mayor takes office.

STORY QUESTIONS

1. Why is Wickam City a wonderful place to live?
2. Why do people enjoy going to the mountains and the beach?
3. Why doesn't Wickam City get more tourist business?

Of all the people in Wickam City, no one enjoys the beach more than Peter Smith. He goes to the beach every weekend. Last Sunday, Peter and Maria got in Peter's sports car and drove to Sunset Beach. Maria complained.

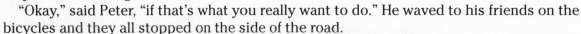

"Every weekend we do the same thing. Why don't we do something different for a change?"

"Sure," said Peter. "But what?"

Just then they passed Otis and Gloria, who were on their bicycles. Maria waved to them from the car.

"I know," said Maria. "Let's exchange the car for the bicycles! Otis and Gloria will enjoy driving a sports car, and we'll enjoy riding bicycles for a change."

"Okay," said Peter, "if that's what you really want to do." He waved to his friends on the bicycles and they all stopped on the side of the road.

After talking for a while, they all agreed that Maria's idea could be fun. They decided to meet at the beach and have lunch together at the Seahorse Restaurant.

"We'll see you there!" they all said to each other. Peter and Maria watched Otis and Gloria drive the car down the road and disappear.

"I think we'll get there faster if we take this side road through the hills," said Peter. "We might even get to the beach before them." They began pedaling the bikes up the hill.

After a while, Maria began to complain. "This is hard work," she said. "I'm tired."

Peter agreed. He was hot and sweaty. His legs ached. He didn't enjoy riding a bicycle at all. Soon they were too tired to pedal, and they had to get off and push the bikes. After what seemed like hours, they finally arrived at the beach.

"At least Otis and Gloria had a good time," said Peter. He wiped the sweat from his forehead.

Just then they saw Otis. He looked tired. He was dirty and covered with sweat and grease.

"Am I glad to see you!" he shouted. "Never again! I'm never going to drive a car again."

"Why Otis, what happened?" asked Maria. They stared at Otis.

"First the car ran out of gas," he explained. "I had to walk a mile to get gas. Then the motor stopped. I had to fix it. Finally we had a flat tire. I had to change it. A car is too much trouble. I'd rather ride a bicycle!"

STORY QUESTIONS

1. What did Peter and Maria do last weekend?
2. Do you think Maria enjoys the beach as much as Peter does? Why or why not?
3. What did Maria want to do when she saw Otis and Gloria?
4. Where did they all agree to meet?
5. Why didn't Peter enjoy riding a bicycle?
6. What did Otis say about driving a car?
7. What problems did Otis have with the sports car?
8. What did he have to do?
9. What did Otis and Peter learn from their experience?

FREE RESPONSE

1. Do you live closer to the mountains or the ocean?
2. Describe the area surrounding your city.
3. Does your city get much tourist business? Why or why not?
4. What kind of outdoor activities do people enjoy where you live?
5. What are your favorite outdoor activities?
6. Would you rather go to the beach or to the mountains?
7. Have you ever gone camping or fishing?
8. What can you do in the summer that you can't do in the winter?
9. What do you think is the best way to spend a beautiful summer day?

PAIR WORK • *Ask and answer questions using* ***would rather.***

watch TV or listen to the radio
A: **Would you rather watch TV or listen to the radio?**
B: **I'd rather watch TV.**
   OR **I'd rather listen to the radio.**
   OR **I like both.**

1. sing or dance
2. go to a movie or see a play
3. study at home or in the library
4. listen to classical music or rock
5. talk about sports or politics
6. work in an office or outdoors
7. have a lot of money or a lot of friends
8. live in the city or in the country

PRACTICE • *Combine the sentences using* ***too.***

I'm very tired. I can't finish my homework.
I'm too tired to finish my homework.

She's embarrassed. She won't talk about her problems.
She's too embarrassed to talk about her problems.

1. He's lazy. He won't do any work.
2. He's cheap. He won't take his girlfriend to a nice restaurant.
3. She's very sophisticated. She would never eat with her fingers.
4. She's very nice. She would never tell her boyfriend he has bad taste.
5. He's very proud. He would never ask her for money.
6. She's upset. She can't eat her dinner.
7. He's nervous. He can't talk in front of a big crowd.
8. She's frightened. She won't walk home alone.

WRITTEN EXERCISE • *Complete the sentences using the correct form of* **make** *or* **do.**

> The verb **do** often refers to general activity or a certain kind of work.
> The verb **make** often means create or produce.

Mrs. Hamby ___*made*___ a chocolate cake last week.

She's ___*doing*___ the gardening this afternoon.

1. Please be quiet. You're __making__ too much noise.
2. The girls are __doing__ their homework.
3. Mabel __did__ the cleaning yesterday.
4. Sam __did__ $80 a month when he was in the army.
5. Linda always __does__ her best to __make__ a good impression.
6. Nancy was happy that she could __do__ something to help Otis.
7. Have you __don__ the shopping?
8. Mrs. Hamby is going to __make__ sandwiches for lunch.
9. I'm __making__ plans for the future.
10. We hope to __do__ a lot of business in New York.
11. Mr. Bascomb has __made__ several speeches this week.
12. He can't __do__ anything without our support.

PRACTICE • *Make conclusions using* **want** + *object* + *infinitive.*

> Suzanne is giving Nick her phone number. **She wants him to call her.**
>
> Peter thinks Maria works too hard. **He wants her to relax and enjoy life.**

1. Mona is unhappy because Fred is unemployed.
2. She's complaining because he left his dirty dishes in the sink.
3. Mr. Hamby thinks his wife is getting too fat.
4. Maria is afraid because Peter is driving too fast.
5. Barney can't sleep because his neighbors are making too much noise.
6. Mrs. Mango is upset because her son, Marty, gets poor grades in school.
7. Mr. Brown is worried about his wife's health.
8. Gloria misses her brother. She hasn't seen him for a long while.
9. Barbara is unhappy because Tino is taking a long time to get ready.
10. Miss Moneypenny is broke. She's talking to her rich uncle now.

PAIR WORK • *Ask your partner these questions: What do your family and friends want you to do? Why do they want you to do these things? What do you want your family and friends to do? Why?*

In recent years, the fitness movement has been gaining popularity all over the world. Health clubs, exercise classes, and bodybuilding centers have sprung up from Tokyo to Rome—and even Moscow. Health magazines, books, records, and videotapes are selling like lemonade on a hot summer day. And yet, despite the fitness boom, there are still many people who are unfit. This includes millions who play tennis, baseball, or football. It includes millions who work out at health clubs, pump iron, or do calisthenics. The problem is, our workouts don't make us sweat enough or breathe hard enough. We don't run far enough or exercise long enough.

We need to put more aerobic training in our lives. Aerobics is the system of exercise first developed by Dr. Kenneth Cooper. It involves moving vigorously and steadily over a period of twenty to forty-five minutes, so that the cardiovascular system (heart, lungs, and circulatory system) works harder and supplies more oxygen to the muscles. When the oxygen reaches the muscles, it combines with fuel sources to produce energy. The more oxygen we can supply to the muscles, the more efficiently the body can utilize this oxygen, and the more physically fit we become.

There are many kinds of exercise that will help us get in shape. Three of the most popular are running, weightlifting, and swimming.

Running. The best aerobic exercise is running, and the best distance runner on this planet is the human animal. Other animals, such as the cheetah, can run faster over short distances, but the human outperforms all other animals of comparable size in long-distance running. It is this extraordinary capacity to run long and hard, even in the heat of day, that made early man a formidable hunter. Anthropologists point out that primitive people, in pursuits lasting up to two days, have outrun many kinds of animals known for their great speed. Tarahumara Indians, for example, chase deer through the mountains of northern Mexico until the animals collapse from exhaustion.

Humans are the best distance runners because we have the most efficient sweat glands in the animal kingdom; no other species sweats as copiously. Our superior cooling system makes it possible for us to run long distances on hot days. We also have a superior breathing system, enabling us to change speeds without losing efficiency. And our diet, which includes carbohydrates, allows us to store energy longer than carnivores and most other animals. All this adds up to one simple fact: we were born to run, especially to run long distances.

Weight-training. Although running is an excellent aerobic exercise, it isn't enough for total fitness. If you want to put on muscle and get stronger, the best way to do it is through weight-training. Lifting weights can make your muscles larger, firmer, and stronger. And it doesn't take very long—most people begin to see changes in the mirror within a week or so of first laying hands on iron.

Before starting a weight-training program, everyone should have some instruction. The most important thing is to take it easy at the beginning. Start with moderate weights and take a little more time. Showing off, even to yourself, how much you can lift is the easiest way to hurt yourself. As you improve, you can increase the weight and the number of repetitions. And pay attention to form. Good form will help protect you from injury.

In the past, weight-lifting was primarily an activity for men, but today thousands of women are pumping iron in gyms all over the world. Women are discovering that lifting weights has many benefits. It makes them healthier, stronger, and more energetic, and it gives them a feeling of power.

Swimming. For all-around fitness, there's no sport that can take the place of swimming. Swimming builds up your limbs, heart, and lungs. It improves coordination and strength, and for aerobic benefit it is almost as good as running. There's very little risk of injury, and it's an activity you will probably never grow too old to do. Some people enjoy swimming because it gives them a feeling of peace. They enter a cool, wet world where there are no distractions—no one to listen to and no one to argue with. This solitude can be the most pleasant part of swimming, a chance to let the mind relax as the body works, a time to relieve stress and work off tension. What's more, swimming can build your self-esteem and help you sleep better at night.

In spite of all the benefits we get from exercise, there are still many people who don't like to work out. Ask them why they don't exercise and they might say that running, calisthenics, and weight-training are boring. Or that they are too busy. But a good exercise program doesn't have to take up a lot of time, and it can be a lot of fun. Working out is good for the mind as well as the body. When we are in shape, we feel good about ourselves and are less likely to suffer from depression. Regular exercise not only makes us look and feel better, it can actually defend us from illness and prolong our lives.

1. What are some of the benefits of exercise?
2. How is it possible for some people to play sports and still be out of shape?
3. What does aerobic exercise do for the human body?
4. What is the best aerobic exercise?
5. Which animal is the best long-distance runner on the planet?
6. What advantages do humans have when it comes to long-distance running?
7. What is weight-training good for?
8. What things should you keep in mind when you start a weight-training program?
9. Why is weight training becoming more popular among women?
10. What is the best sport for all-around fitness?
11. What are some of the benefits of swimming?
12. What are some excuses people give for not exercising?
13. How often do you exercise? What's your favorite kind of exercise?

PAST TENSE HAVE TO
Affirmative

He They	had to	wait. pay.

Negative

He They	didn't have to	wait. pay.

Interrogative

Did	he they	have to	wait? pay?

Short Answers

Yes,	he they	did.

No,	he they	didn't.

FUTURE TENSE HAVE TO
Affirmative

We You	will have to	wait. pay.

Negative

We You	won't have to	wait. pay.

Interrogative

Will	we you	have to	wait? pay?

Short Answers

Yes,	we you	will.

No,	we you	won't.

VERB + OBJECT + INFINITIVE (with TO)

They	asked invited wanted allowed expected	her	to go to the party.

I	showed taught	him	how to use a camera. how to play the guitar.

WOULD RATHER

Would you rather	watch TV or listen to the radio? play tennis or go to a movie?

I'd rather	listen to the radio than watch TV. play tennis than go to a movie.

Chapter

TOPICS
Places to live
Juvenile delinquency
Work

GRAMMAR
Second conditional
So + adjective/such + noun
Reflexive pronouns

FUNCTIONS
Expressing possibility and probability
Making wishes
Talking about consequences
Giving advice
Persuading

1

2

1. *Talk about the pictures.*
2. *Listen to the stories.*
3. *Answer the story questions.*

READING

1 Sam and Mabel Brown wish they lived on a farm. If they had a farm, they could raise animals and produce their own food. It's hard work, but Mr. and Mrs. Brown would enjoy the peace and quiet of being in the country. And they could spend more time with their children. Linda could have her own horse, and Jimmy could go hunting and fishing with his father. On the other hand, if the Browns left Wickam City, Jimmy and Linda wouldn't be able to finish college and they would miss their friends. The Browns almost bought a farm several months ago, but it wasn't what they expected. Nowadays, it's hard to find a good piece of farmland at a reasonable price.

1. Where do Sam and Mabel wish they lived?
2. What could they do if they had a farm?
3. What could Jimmy and Linda do if they lived on a farm?
4. What would Jimmy and Linda miss if they left Wickam City?
5. How is life in the country different from life in the city?

2 Elmer and Sarah Coggins have lived on a farm most of their lives, and it hasn't been easy. In 1989 their house burned down. This year they have lost most of their corn and wheat crops due to bad weather. As if that weren't bad enough, last month Nancy Paine crashed into their barn. Sarah Coggins thinks it would be better if they moved to the city. Elmer could get a job working in his brother's supermarket, and she could open a bakery. She makes wonderful cakes and pies. If Elmer and Sarah moved to the city, they would make new friends and go out more often. But they would probably miss their farm. After all, it's the only life they have ever known.

1. How would you describe Elmer and Sarah's life on the farm?
2. What are some of the unfortunate things that have happened to them?
3. What does Sarah think they should do?
4. Where could Elmer get a job?
5. What could Sarah do?
6. Do you think Elmer and Sarah should stay on the farm or move to the city? Why?

SECOND CONDITIONAL

If they lived on a farm, they could raise animals.

_____, _____ produce their own food.

_____, _____ go hunting and fishing.

_____, _____ spend more time with their children.

PRACTICE • *Make sentences using the second conditional with* **could.**

They don't live on a farm, so they can't produce their own food.
If they lived on a farm, they could produce their own food.

She doesn't have any flour, so she can't make a cake.
If she had some flour, she could make a cake.

1. He doesn't know her address, so he can't send her a letter.
2. They don't have any money, so they can't go to a movie.
3. We don't have a car, so we can't drive to the beach.
4. He doesn't know how to swim, so he can't go in the water.
5. I don't have my watch, so I can't tell you the time.
6. She doesn't live near her job, so she can't walk to work.
7. He doesn't own any property, so he can't get a loan from the bank.
8. We don't have their telephone number, so we can't call them.

Listen and practice.

SARAH: This farm is too much trouble, Elmer. I wish we could sell it and move to the city.

ELMER: What would we do in the city? Farming is the only life we know.

SARAH: You could work for your brother. He'd give you a job.

ELMER: No thanks. I couldn't stand working in a supermarket.

SARAH: Oh, it wouldn't be so bad, Elmer. And think of me. I could start a bakery with the money we'd get from this farm.

ELMER: You'd get homesick for this old place, Sarah. And you'd miss all your friends. I know you.

SARAH: We could make new friends in the city. There would be more places to go and things to do. We'd have a great time.

ELMER: Oh boy, the grass is always greener on the other side of the fence!

SARAH: Well, sometimes it is. You never know until you try.

ELMER: This is a big decision, Sarah. We'd better think about it some more first.

SECOND CONDITIONAL

If they left the farm, they would have to find new jobs.

_____, _____ live in a smaller house.

_____, _____ miss their friends.

_____, _____ get homesick.

The if-clause states an action that is not likely to happen. However, if the action in the if-clause happened, it is quite probable that the action in the result clause would happen. We often use the second conditional to talk about imaginary situations.

PRACTICE 1 • *Make sentences using the second conditional with **would**.*

They don't work fast, so they won't finish today.
If they worked fast, they would finish today.

It isn't raining, so I won't take my umbrella.
If it were raining, I would take my umbrella.

1. He doesn't want to be a doctor, so he won't study medicine.
2. She doesn't love him, so she won't marry him.
3. They aren't in a hurry, so they won't take a taxi.
4. We aren't hungry, so we won't eat now.
5. This book isn't interesting, so I won't finish reading it.
6. He doesn't study, so he won't pass the test.
7. She doesn't respect him, so she won't take his advice.
8. They don't practice, so they won't improve.
9. I don't like them, so I won't help them.

PRACTICE 2 • *Make affirmative sentences using **wish**.*

You don't read many books.
I wish you read more books.

He doesn't speak English.
I wish he spoke English.

She doesn't study very much.
I wish she studied more.

1. He doesn't exercise very much.
2. She doesn't like classical music.
3. They don't have a car.
4. I don't have much free time.
5. We don't go out very often.
6. He doesn't help us very much.
7. She doesn't write many letters.
8. They don't understand.
9. I don't know the answer.

PRACTICE 3 • *Make negative sentences using **wish**.*

My car makes a lot of noise.
I wish it didn't make so much noise.

Your sister asks too many questions.
I wish she didn't ask so many questions.

I get bored very easily.
I wish I didn't get bored so easily.

1. She talks too much.
2. He works very slowly.
3. They spend a lot of money.
4. You drive very fast.
5. We make too many mistakes.
6. He watches a lot of television.
7. I get tired very easily.
8. You eat too many pastries.
9. She wastes a lot of time.

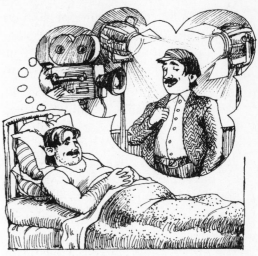

1. *Talk about the pictures.*
2. *Listen to the story.*
3. *Answer the story questions.*

READING

Barney made quite an impression on Ula Hackey, the famous Hollywood actress, when they met a couple of weeks ago. She thought Barney had such an interesting personality that he would make a good actor. She even offered him a part in her new movie, called *High Times*. She wanted Barney to play the part of a taxi driver.

Barney loved the idea of being in the movies and told all his friends about it. He was so excited that he couldn't sleep at night. He lay awake thinking about his future in Hollywood. Barney started seeing Miss Hackey at the hotel where she was staying, and they talked about his part in the film. She gave him a script so he could study his lines at home. Barney was such a good student that he memorized his part in less than a week. Miss Hackey was so pleased with his progress that she decided to leave for Hollywood right away and take Barney with her.

Everything went perfectly until the second day of filming, when Barney had his first big scene. It was such a hot day that everyone on the set was uncomfortable. The director didn't like Barney because he wasn't a professional actor. He yelled at Barney several times. Barney was so nervous that he could hardly talk. He forgot his lines and started shaking. He was so discouraged that he felt like quitting. Ula Hackey came over and tried to cheer him up. She understood how Barney felt.

1. Why did Ula Hackey think Barney would make a good actor?
2. What part did she want him to play in her new movie?
3. Was Barney excited about being in the movies?
4. How long did it take Barney to learn his lines?
5. What did Miss Hackey do after Barney memorized his part?
6. Why was everyone uncomfortable on the second day of filming?
7. How did the director treat Barney?
8. How did Barney feel?
9. What did Ula Hackey do?

SO...THAT

He was so nervous that he could hardly talk.

_____ forgot his lines.

_____ started shaking.

_____ wanted to go home.

PRACTICE • *Combine the sentences using so . . . that.*

This coffee is very hot. I can't drink it.
This coffee is so hot (that) I can't drink it.

1. Linda is very tired. She can't finish her homework.
2. Mr. Bascomb is very busy. He can't leave the office.
3. This box is very heavy. I can't lift it.
4. Mr. Twaddle is very short. He can't reach the window.
5. He's very poor. He can't buy a new pair of shoes.
6. His bed is very uncomfortable. He can't sleep in it.
7. The bus is very crowded. Mrs. Golo can't find a seat.
8. She's very boring. I can't listen to her.

Listen and practice.

BARNEY: Oh, Miss Hackey, I was so nervous I couldn't remember my lines.

ULA: Don't feel bad, Barney. It could happen to anyone. This is only your first experience.

BARNEY: Do you think I'll ever be a good actor?

ULA: Sure. You've got so much talent you can't miss. But first you've got to think of yourself as an actor, a real professional.

BARNEY: The director didn't treat me like a professional. He was shouting at me so much I couldn't concentrate.

ULA: He had no right to do that. But it's such a hot day that everyone's a little on edge. The director got excited and lost his temper, that's all.

BARNEY: Does he always get mad at the actors?

ULA: No, he's usually a good man to work with. But he's got a tough job. If anything goes wrong, the director gets the blame.

BARNEY: I never thought of that.

ULA: Sure. Put yourself in his shoes. It isn't easy directing a movie like this.

BARNEY: I suppose you're right. I was just feeling sorry for myself. Please be patient with me.

ULA: Don't worry, Barney. Everything will be OK.

SUCH ... THAT

She was such a nice person that she never got mad.

_____ raised her voice.

_____ lost her temper.

_____ had any problems.

PRACTICE • *Combine the sentences using **such ... that.***

It was a very interesting movie. I saw it twice.
It was such an interesting movie (that) I saw it twice.

He's having a good time. He doesn't want to go home.
He's having such a good time (that) he doesn't want to go home.

1. She has a nice personality. Everyone likes her.
2. We were having a pleasant talk. I didn't want to leave.
3. Dr. Pasto is an intelligent man. Everyone listens to him.
4. He's had an exciting life. He could write a book about it.
5. Anne has a very good voice. She could be a professional singer.
6. She lives in a very small apartment. She can't have visitors.
7. Mr. Bascomb is a very powerful man. Everyone is afraid of him.
8. He's a very busy man. He doesn't have time for his family.

REFLEXIVE PRONOUNS

I was feeling sorry for myself.	We were feeling sorry for ourselves.
He _____ himself.	You _____ yourselves.
She _____ herself.	They _____ themselves.

WRITTEN EXERCISE • *Complete the sentences using reflexive pronouns.*

You've got to think of ___*yourself*___ as an actor.

They introduced ___*themselves*___ right away.

1. I bought ___myself___ a new pair of shoes.
2. She taught ___herself___ to play the guitar.
3. We enjoyed ___ourselves___ at the party.
4. He made ___himselves___ a sandwich.
5. You can all take care of ___yourselves___.
6. She looked at ___herself___ in the mirror.
7. He didn't recognize ___himself___ after he got a haircut.
8. They always talk about ___themselves___.

Fred Farmer has been looking for a job for several months, but he hasn't been able to find anything that suits his personality. He refuses to work in an office, and he can't seem to find any interesting outdoor jobs. Fred has gone to several employment agencies, but they haven't been able to help him. The job situation is very bad in Wickam City.

Fred used to make a little money selling hot dogs at the sports stadium. But he quit when he realized that he was wasting his time doing that kind of work. He knew that he would have to find a regular job. He promised his sister that he wouldn't stop looking until he found something worthwhile. After checking many job possibilities and having no success, he finally decided to get some professional advice. Yesterday he called on Dr. Pasto, a man everyone goes to when they are having problems.

"I know why you've come," said Dr. Pasto in a friendly voice. "You can't decide what to do with your life and you think I can help you. Am I right?"

"Why, yes. But how did you know?"

"You might call it an educated guess," said Dr. Pasto. "But it's not important how I know these things. What is important is that you make something of your life."

"I know sir. But what can I do? I don't have any training, and there aren't any jobs for people without skills."

"You may not have any training to speak of," said Dr. Pasto. "But there must be some kind of work you can do. First, tell me about yourself. What do you do with all that free time you have on your hands?"

"I spend most of my time at the park," said Fred. "I enjoy teaching kids how to play baseball. I used to be a professional baseball player several years ago."

"That's wonderful," said Dr. Pasto. "I'm sure all the boys look up to you."

"I guess so," said Fred, a little embarrassed. "They're a great bunch of kids."

"They're lucky to have someone like you, Fred. There are very few men who are willing to spend so much of their time helping boys in the neighborhood."

"It's the least I can do, sir. Most of the kids come from poor families and some of them don't have fathers. There's nothing for them to do, so they go to the park."

"You've touched on one of our major problems," said Dr. Pasto. "There are too many boys in Wickam City with time on their hands and nothing to do. It's a shame so many of them become juvenile delinquents."

"I got in a lot of trouble myself when I was a kid," said Fred. "There was no one to look after me."

"I'll bet the boys at the park remind you of yourself when you were their age," said Dr. Pasto.

"They sure do, especially one kid named Marty. I know his mother. She works at the ice cream factory. Her husband died a few years ago and Marty really misses his father. So I try and look after the little guy."

"I know who you're talking about," said Dr. Pasto. "He's always getting in trouble. A couple of weeks ago I caught him in the backyard of my house. He was taking apples from my tree."

"I'm sorry to hear that," said Fred. "I hope you got tough with him."

"I sure did," said Dr. Pasto. "But I wasn't nearly as angry as he thought I was. I really sympathize with Marty. I know he's having a tough time. His teacher, Mrs. Golo, told me about him. She said he isn't doing well in school and has no respect for authority."

"I guess I'm the only one he listens to," said Fred. "I get along well with boys like Marty because we have fun together."

"You're probably the only one who takes a real interest in them. Everyone else is too busy. You know, Fred, you're doing a real service to the community by giving so much of your time to these boys. If more people did the same, we wouldn't have a problem with gangs."

"I suppose you're right, Dr. Pasto. I only wish I could do more."

"You can, Fred. Have you ever thought about starting a club for boys?"

"That's a great idea. But I'm not sure I could do it by myself. It's a big job."

"Have a little faith in yourself," said Dr. Pasto. "You can do it."

"I'm willing to try. But it takes a lot of money to start a boys' club, and I'm broke."

"Why don't you talk to Otis Jackson about it? He's concerned about the youth in our town. If he wins the election for mayor, he'll be able to help you get the money."

"You're right. Otis is the man to see. I'm going to talk to him as soon as possible. Thanks very much for your advice, Dr. Pasto. You've really helped me. From now on, I'm going to make the most of my life."

"That's wonderful, Fred. Good-bye and good luck to you."

STORY QUESTIONS

1. What is Fred's problem?
2. Who did he go to for advice?
3. Why is it difficult for a man like Fred to find a job?
4. What does Fred do with his free time?
5. What often happens to boys with time on their hands and nothing to do?
6. Why does Fred try to look after Marty?
7. How did Marty get into trouble with Dr. Pasto?
8. Why does Fred get along well with boys like Marty?
9. How could Fred do more to help boys in the neighborhood?
10. Why can't Fred start a boys' club by himself?
11. Why did Dr. Pasto ask Fred to talk to Otis Jackson?
12. Who do you go to when you need help or advice?

PAIR WORK • *You're having problems. Your partner gives you advice.*

A: **I'm broke.**
B: **If I were you, I'd work harder.**
   OR **If I were you, I'd save my money.**
   OR **If I were you, I wouldn't spend so much.**

1. I'm working too hard.
2. My salary is too low.
3. I don't like my job.
4. My car isn't running very well.
5. My shoes are worn out.
6. I'm bored.
7. I'm out of shape.
8. I have a headache.
9. My neighbors make too much noise.
10. I don't have enough money to pay the rent.

Albert got very hungry. He went home and made five sandwiches.

He got so hungry (that) he went home and made five sandwiches.

He ate too much. He couldn't get up from the table.

He ate so much (that) he couldn't get up from the table.

1. Our friends live far away. We can't see them very often.

2. My sister talks very fast. No one can understand her.

3. Mr. Bascomb meets a lot of people. He can't remember all their names.

4. He works too much. He doesn't have time for his family.

5. He was very tired last night. He went to bed right after dinner.

6. He worries a lot. He can't sleep at night.

7. It was raining very hard yesterday. We couldn't go outside.

8. We ate too much candy. We got sick.

9. Barney tells a lot of stories. I can't remember them all.

10. He enjoys acting very much. He doesn't want to drive a taxi anymore.

PAIR WORK • *Have conversations using reflexive pronouns.*

> A: **Did Linda make that dress?**
> B: **Yes, she made it herself.**
> A: **Did you fix up the living room?**
> B: **Yes, I fixed it up myself.**

1. Did Peter repair his car?
2. Did Barbara and Tino paint their house?
3. Did Nancy fix her TV set?
4. Did Jimmy plan the party?
5. Did you make the cake?
6. Did the women pay for their vacation?
7. Did Mr. Bascomb write that speech?
8. Did Anne carry those boxes?
9. Did the boys plant the apple tree?
10. Did you cut your hair?

FREE RESPONSE

1. What would you do if you saw a fire?
2. What would you do if you saw a robbery?
3. What would you do if you saw an automobile accident?
4. What would you do if a stranger asked you for money?
5. What would you do if you lost all your money?
6. What would you do if you got bad service in a restaurant?
7. What would you do if you found a camera in the park?
8. What would you do if you couldn't sleep at night?
9. What would you do if your best friend got sick?
10. What would you do if you had more free time?

GROUP WORK • *If you could have three wishes, what would they be? How would your life be different if your wishes came true? Write down your wishes and discuss them with the group.*

> **I wish I had more free time.**
> **I wish I lived in a bigger house.**
> **I wish I could play the piano.**

DISCUSSION • *Is it always a good thing to have your wishes come true? Is it possible for a person to have a lot of money and possessions and still be unhappy? What do you think are the most important things in life?*

Aladdin and the Magic Lamp

Working for pay is the common experience of people all over the world, since everyone must work in order to have a decent life. However, there are considerable differences in people's salaries and in their attitudes toward work: Some people like their jobs and some don't. For people to be happy at work, they must earn a decent salary and feel that they are making the best use of their talents and abilities. They should also feel that their work is valuable, that it benefits society in some way.

When people are dissatisfied, it's often because they have jobs that give them little opportunity to advance or develop their potential. In many cases, they have chosen the wrong profession. To avoid this mistake, the first thing people need to do is identify their strengths. Then they can determine the kind of work that is best for them. If, for example, a young woman is good at drawing, she might think of becoming a commercial artist or designer. To prepare herself for one of these careers, she would probably study for four years at an art institute or university. For most people, this step is the most difficult—getting the education and training that will enable them to enter the field they are interested in. It is often necessary to study long and hard to enter certain professions, and some people are not willing to make the sacrifice. With work, as with most things in life, nothing worthwhile comes easily.

Now, there are certain people who are addicted to their work. They only think about their jobs, even when they aren't working. These people are known as "workaholics." Workaholics seldom take time to play and have fun because they are "married" to their jobs. When they take vacations, they take "working" vacations. And they often say things like "time is money" and "business before pleasure." Workaholics are usually successful in their careers, but they often have dull personalities and aren't much fun to be with. So they pay a price for their success. For people to be successful *and* happy, they must have a balance in their lives between work and play. They must have jobs in which they can develop their talents and abilities, and enough free time to enjoy family and friends.

1. Why is work important?
2. Do you think most people are satisfied with their jobs? Why or why not?
3. Do you think it's necessary for people to like their jobs in order to be happy?
4. How can you determine which job is best for you?
5. Do you think it's worth making sacrifices today in order to live better tomorrow?
6. Which would you rather have: an interesting job that pays an average salary, or a boring job that pays a high salary?
7. Would you work if you didn't have to? Why?
8. What is a "workaholic"?
9. What price do workaholics pay for their success?
10. What do people need in order to be successful and happy?
11. Do you have a balance in your life between work and play?
12. What kinds of activities do you enjoy with your family and friends?

TALKING ABOUT PLACES TO LIVE

Some people who live on farms would like to live in the city, and vice versa. People often think the grass is greener on the other side of the fence.

1. Where would you rather live: on a farm or in the city?
2. What are the advantages of living on a farm?
3. What are the advantages of living in the city?
4. If you could live anywhere in the world, where would you like to live? Why do you think you would enjoy living there?
5. What do you like about the area where you are living now? What are some of the things you don't like?
6. Do you know any places that are nice to visit but where you wouldn't want to live?
7. Have you ever been away from home for a long time? Were you homesick? What did you miss the most?

ROLE PLAY

Student A plays the part of a young husband. Student B plays his wife.

Situation: The husband has been offered a higher-paying job in another city. But his wife likes the city they are living in now, and she doesn't want to leave her friends. He points out the advantages of moving, and she gives her reasons for wanting to stay.

TALKING ABOUT JUVENILE DELINQUENCY

Juvenile delinquency is becoming a serious problem in Wickam City as more young people are getting into trouble with the law.

1. What are some of the reasons for juvenile delinquency? Do you think parents are responsible?
2. What are some of the most common juvenile crimes?
3. How can we deal with the problem of juvenile crime? What can we do to help young people?
4. What kinds of youth organizations does your town have? What kinds of activities do they sponsor?
5. How can young people earn money? What kinds of jobs are available to them?

GROUP WORK • *Discuss the major problems that affect young people in your community. Which problem do you think is the most serious? What can be done about it? Share your findings with the class.*

COMPOSITION

1. Write about juvenile delinquency. What are the causes? What can be done about it?
2. If you could live anywhere in the world, where would you live? Give your reasons.

VOCABULARY

authority	faith	memorize	skill	yell (v.)
		miss (v.)	stranger (n.)	yourself
bakery	gang (n.)		sympathize	youth
		own (adj.)		
check (v.)	holiday (n.)		talent	
community		pie	touch (v.)	
concentrate	juvenile (adj.)	possibility	tough (adj.)	
	juvenile delinquent	produce (v.)	training (n.)	
decent				
due	line (n.)	robbery	wheat	
		rough (adj.)	wish (v.)	
especially			worthwhile	
			wrong (adj.)	

EXPRESSIONS

I was feeling sorry for myself.
Put yourself in his shoes.
It's the least I can do.
It could happen to anyone.

He has no training to speak of.
He has a lot of time on his hands.
He would make a good actor.
He felt like quitting.
He lost his temper.
He had no right to do that.

Please be patient.
Have faith in yourself.
Oh boy!
It hasn't been easy.
Everything went perfectly.

to be pleased
to be discouraged
to be broke
to be on edge
to be willing

to lay awake
to look after someone
to look up to someone
to take an interest in someone

Don't feel bad.
You can't miss.
Think of me.
You're the boss.

As if that weren't bad enough...
This farm is too much trouble.
The grass is always greener on the other
     side of the fence.
You never know until you try.
We'd better think about it.

an educated guess
on the other hand
due to bad weather
from now on
vice versa

to get excited
to get mad
to get tough
to get the blame
to get homesick

GRAMMAR SUMMARY

SECOND CONDITIONAL with COULD

If	we had a car,	we could drive to the beach.
	you knew their address,	you could send them a letter.
	she practiced,	she could be a good tennis player.

SECOND CONDITIONAL with WOULD

If	he studied,	he would pass the test.
	I were you,	I would take the bus.
	they left the farm,	they would miss their friends.

My car makes a lot of noise.
I don't know how to fix it.

WISH

I wish	it didn't make so much noise.
	I knew how to fix it.

SO ... (THAT)

This coffee is	so	hot	(that)	I can't drink it.
He played		well		he won every game.

SUCH ... (THAT)

It was	such	an interesting movie	(that)	I saw it twice.
She has		a friendly personality		everyone likes her.

REFLEXIVE PRONOUNS

Singular	Plural
myself	ourselves
yourself	yourselves
himself	
herself	themselves
itself	

AFTER CERTAIN VERBS

He asked himself the same question.
We enjoyed ourselves at the party.
She introduced herself to me.

FOR EMPHASIS

She wanted to see Dr. Pasto himself.
I got into trouble myself when I was a boy.
They painted the house themselves.

AFTER PREPOSITIONS

Can you laugh at yourself?
They always talk about themselves.
He said something to himself.

Chapter

7

TOPICS
Housing
The legal system
Dreams

GRAMMAR
Gerunds

FUNCTIONS
Criticizing
Asking for and giving directions
Telling a story
Describing people
Talking about dreams
Renting an apartment

1. *Talk about the pictures.*

 2. *Listen to the story.*

3. *Answer the story questions.*

Ben Fix used to be a real estate agent. He got rich by selling worthless farmland to people from the city who didn't know what they were buying. He was very good at fooling the public. Mr. Fix used the money he got from selling farmland to buy an old apartment building in Wickam City. It was called the Bedford Arms. Most of the tenants were senior citizens who had low incomes and were used to paying low rents. Mr. Fix wanted to make a few minor improvements and then charge high rents, but first he had to get rid of the people living there. He chose to do this by making life miserable for everyone in the building. He drew up a long list of unnecessary regulations and insisted that everyone obey them. Anyone who broke the rules had to move out of the building.

Mr. Fix would do anything to get what he wanted. At times he even cut off the electricity and said he was doing it to save energy. The tenants complained, but it was no use. Mr. Fix always defended his actions and told the tenants to leave if they weren't happy. After a while, they got tired of living under these conditions and started moving out. They weren't used to dealing with a man like Mr. Fix. He almost succeeded in driving everyone out of the building, but he didn't count on the opposition he got from one of his tenants, an old lady named Olive Grove. She wouldn't give up without a fight and even went to see the public defender, Justin Case.

1. Did Mr. Fix used to be a banker or a real estate agent?
2. How did he get rich?
3. What did he buy with the money he got from selling farmland?
4. Why did Mr. Fix want the tenants to leave the building?
5. What did he do to get rid of them?
6. What happened when they complained?
7. Did Mr. Fix succeed in driving everyone out of the building? Why not?

USED TO Affirmative	USED TO Negative
They were used to paying low rents.	They weren't used to dealing with a man like Mr. Fix.
_____ having visitors.	_____ having problems with the owner.
_____ seeing their friends.	_____ living with a lot of regulations.
_____ living peacefully.	_____ paying high rents.

PRACTICE • *Make true sentences about yourself using **used to.***

eat alone
I'm used to eating alone. I do it all the time.
OR **I'm not used to eating alone. I usually eat with my family.**

1. get up early
2. take a cold shower
3. have a big breakfast
4. drink coffee
5. take the bus
6. work hard
7. do the shopping
8. cook dinner
9. wash the dishes
10. go to bed early

Listen and practice.

OLIVE GROVE: Hello, Mr. Case. My name is Olive Grove.

JUSTIN CASE: Yes, ma'am. What can I do for you?

OLIVE GROVE: I've got a serious problem, Mr. Case. The owner of the apartment building where I live is trying to force all the tenants out. I'm afraid of losing my apartment.

JUSTIN CASE: Why does the owner want you people out of the building?

OLIVE GROVE: He thinks we're paying too little rent. We've all been there for a long time, so our rents are fairly low. The owner wants to get new tenants and charge them high rents.

JUSTIN CASE: Yes, that makes sense. According to law he can only raise the rent 10 percent a year. He has to wait until someone moves out before he can raise the rent substantially.

OLIVE GROVE: He's only interested in making money, Mr. Case. And he's responsible for causing a lot of unhappiness.

JUSTIN CASE: Can you be more specific, ma'am? Has he done anything that's illegal?

OLIVE GROVE: I don't know what's legal or illegal. But I do know he's done a lot of things that aren't right. He's made a list of rules that are impossible to keep, so he has an excuse to throw people out.

JUSTIN CASE: That's terrible. Is there anything else, ma'am?

OLIVE GROVE: Yes, he doesn't keep up the building, and sometimes he even cuts off the electricity.

JUSTIN CASE:	He should be ashamed of himself. Who is this scoundrel?
OLIVE GROVE:	His name is Mr. Fix. He's a very dishonest man. But he's clever.
JUSTIN CASE:	Don't worry. I'm used to dealing with people like that.
OLIVE GROVE:	Do you think we can stop him, Mr. Case?
JUSTIN CASE:	Sure. We'll take him to court and teach him a lesson. He'll be sorry when we get through with him.
OLIVE GROVE:	Oh, Mr. Case, I'm so glad I came to see you. Thank you very much.
JUSTIN CASE:	That's quite all right. Please call me next week. Goodbye, ma'am.

PREPOSITION + GERUND

He's concerned with making money.
_____ interested in _____.
_____ capable of _____.
_____ good at _____.
_____ fond of _____.

PRACTICE • *Make sentences using gerunds.*

> Mr. Fix is supposed to take care of the building.   (responsible for)
> **He's responsible for taking care of the building.**
>
> Olive doesn't want to lose her apartment.   (afraid of)
> **She's afraid of losing her apartment.**

1. My sister regrets that she caused so much trouble.   (sorry for)
2. She doesn't like to work late.   (tired of)
3. Jimmy wants to study medicine.   (interested in)
4. He likes to repair things.   (good at)
5. Barbara can run a mile in five minutes.   (capable of)
6. We have to take out the trash.   (responsible for)
7. I don't like to drive that old car.   (ashamed of)
8. Jenny and Marty like to eat ice cream.   (fond of)
9. They can't wait to go to the movies.   (excited about)

1. Talk about the pictures.
2. Listen to the story.
3. Answer the story questions.

READING

After talking to Justin Case, Olive Grove went back to the Bedford Arms and called a meeting of all the tenants who were still living in the building. She told them there would be a trial, and they would have the opportunity to settle their differences with Mr. Fix once and for all. Everyone was very excited about the news. They held a long discussion and then drew up a petition listing their complaints. The tenants objected to Mr. Fix:

(1) raising the rent without making necessary improvements in the building;
(2) forcing people out of their apartments for not obeying the new rules;
(3) "saving energy" by cutting off the electricity; and
(4) making money on property while doing nothing to maintain it.

The tenants accused Mr. Fix of discriminating against pet owners and families with children. They also criticized him for being an absentee landlord who was only interested in making money. The next morning they took their petition to Mr. Case, who studied it carefully and then asked them several questions about Mr. Fix. While this was going on, Mr. Fix was talking to his own lawyer, a man named Duke. Both sides thought they had a good chance of getting a favorable decision.

When the trial took place, the courtroom was full of people, including reporters from the local newspapers and radio stations. The trial was short but very exciting. Mr. Duke made several good points in defense of his client. However, Justin Case seemed to have the strongest arguments. After listening to both sides, the judge made his decision. There was absolute silence in the courtroom as he stood up to speak.

1. Where did Olive Grove go after talking to Mr. Case?
2. What did she tell the tenants at the Bedford Arms?
3. Did the tenants draw up a petition, or a new list of rules?
4. What did they object to Mr. Fix doing?
5. Where did they take their petition?
6. Who was Mr. Duke?
7. Did he do a good job of defending Mr. Fix?
8. Who had the strongest arguments: Mr. Duke or Justin Case?

PRACTICE • *Complete each sentence with the most appropriate phrase. Then read each sentence aloud.*

1. The tenants criticized Mr. Fix	for spending too much money.
2. Mr. Fix criticized his tenants	for not doing their homework.
3. We criticized our neighbors	for raising the rent.
4. Mr. Farley criticized his wife	for coming to work late.
5. Mrs. Farley criticized her husband	for not obeying the rules.
6. The students criticized their teacher	for playing loud music.
7. The teacher criticized the students	for not taking out the trash.
8. Mr. Bascomb criticized his employees	for giving them too much homework.

GROUP WORK • *Tell the others about a time you criticized someone. Tell them about a time someone criticized you.*

Listen and practice.

JUDGE: The court finds the defendant, Mr. Fix, guilty of violating his tenant's right to fair housing.

Mr. Fix, you have tried to benefit yourself by forcing people out of their apartments. You have broken the law and for this you must suffer the consequences.

I hereby order you to pay court costs for both sides in this trial. You have 180 days to make all necessary improvements in the Bedford Arms, and in the future you will maintain your property according to the building code. You will not raise the rent more than 5 percent a year and you will respect the rights of your tenants, including pet owners and families with children.

If, for any reason, you should fail to comply with these orders, the court will fine you $5,000. Do you have anything to say for yourself, Mr. Fix?

MR. FIX: Yes, your honor. This trial has really taught me a lesson. I didn't realize until now how badly I was treating the tenants. I want to apologize for causing them so much trouble. I'll try to be a good landlord in the future.

JUDGE: I'm glad to hear you say that, Mr. Fix. Ladies and gentlemen, this trial is over.

DIALOGUE QUESTIONS

1. Did the court find Mr. Fix innocent or guilty?
2. How did Mr. Fix break the law?
3. What did the judge order Mr. Fix to do?
4. Do you think the judge was too hard on Mr. Fix?
5. What will happen to Mr. Fix if he doesn't obey the judge's orders?
6. Why was Mr. Fix so apologetic?
7. Do you think he will be a good landlord in the future?

🔊 *Listen and practice.*

OLIVE GROVE: We won, we won! Mr. Case, I'm so happy I feel like celebrating.

JUSTIN CASE: If you have a party, I hope you'll invite me.

OLIVE GROVE: Of course, Mr. Case. You'll be the guest of honor. We'll have a big celebration at the Bedford Arms.

JUSTIN CASE: That's wonderful. I'll look forward to seeing you there. Oh, and don't forget to invite Mr. Fix!

PREPOSITION + GERUND

They're talking about having a party.

_____ thinking of _____.

_____ planning on _____.

_____ looking forward to _____.

PRACTICE • *Make sentences using gerunds.*

Mr. Fix might make some improvements in the building.   (think about)
He's thinking about making some improvements in the building.

The tenants don't like to pay high rents.   (object to)
They object to paying high rents.

1. Olive would like to celebrate.   (plan on)
2. We're sorry that we made so much noise.   (apologize for)
3. I have to see your brother.   (insist on)
4. He refuses to ask for help.   (be against)
5. He likes to be independent.   (believe in)
6. Mr. Hamby wants to sell his house.   (plan on)
7. He's going to live in Spain.   (look forward to)
8. Anne might leave her job.   (think about)
9. She doesn't like to take orders from Mr. Bascomb.   (object to)
10. He thinks it's necessary to work hard.   (believe in)
11. Mabel doesn't like to get up early.   (complain about)
12. She doesn't like to do the housework.   (put off)

The other day Barbara was walking in the park when she saw Anne Jones sitting by herself on a bench. Something was wrong with Anne. She was looking down at the ground while covering her face with her hands.

"Why are you crying, Anne?" asked Barbara.

"I'm crying because of a dream I had last night."

"Well, tell me about it," said Barbara, sitting down next to her friend.

Anne took in a deep breath and began her story. "It was wonderful, Barbara," she sobbed. "I dreamed that I was at a party and someone asked me to sing."

"That sounds nice, Anne. Then what happened?"

"I sang and played the guitar. Everyone applauded and said I was great. Then a strange man spoke to me and said he was a talent scout for Delta Music. He asked me to go with him for an audition."

Barbara smiled. "That's wonderful, Anne. What happened next?"

"They liked my voice at the music company and recorded one of my songs. It was a surprise success and sold a million copies. I became a star overnight. They asked me to appear on TV and my face was on the cover of *Time* magazine. I traveled all over the country giving concerts and my name was a household word."

"But that's wonderful, Anne. What happened next?"

"A famous director wanted me to star in a movie, and an Arabian oil sheikh asked me to marry him."

"How romantic, Anne! But I don't see why you're crying. That was a beautiful dream."

"Don't you see, Barbara, that's just it. The dream was so beautiful, I'm crying because I woke up."

STORY QUESTIONS

1. Who did Barbara see in the park yesterday?
2. Why was Anne crying?
3. Who was the strange man who spoke to Anne at the party?
4. Did he ask Anne to go with him for an audition, or a job interview?
5. What happened after they recorded one of Anne's songs at the music company?
6. Was her face on the cover of *Life* or *Time?*
7. What did the famous director want Anne to do?
8. What about the Arabian oil sheikh?
9. Why was Anne crying after such a beautiful dream?
10. What does Anne's dream tell us about her?

WRITTEN EXERCISE • *Complete the sentences using the correct form of the verb in parentheses.*

She thanked him for ___*cleaning*___ the windows.   (clean)

It's easy for them ___*to make*___ friends.   (make)

1. They decided _____ at seven o'clock.   (leave)

2. You should call before _____ over there.   (go)

3. She plans _____ her mother.   (visit)

4. I'm thinking about _____ my camera.   (sell)

5. We need the lamp for _____ .   (read)

6. He hopes _____ medicine.   (study)

7. She got to be a good tennis player by _____ .   (practice)

8. I was glad I had a chance _____ Dr. Pasto.   (meet)

9. Do you mind _____ outside?   (wait)

10. It's important for us _____ patient.   (be)

11. Don't forget _____ me.   (call)

12. I look forward to _____ you again.   (see)

FREE RESPONSE

1. What do you plan on doing this weekend?
2. What do you feel like doing now?
3. What are some things you look forward to doing?
4. What are some things you dream of doing?
5. What are some things you object to doing or put off doing?
6. What are some things you benefit from doing?
7. What are some things you don't believe in doing?
8. What are some things you are tired of doing?
9. What are some things you are afraid of doing?
10. What are some things you are good at doing?

CLASS ACTIVITY • *What are these people dreaming about?*

1. Barney is dreaming that he is riding in a convertible with Ula Hackey. Barney is a big Hollywood producer, and Ula Hackey is crazy about him. Everywhere they go, people smile and wave to them.

1. Barney

2. Gladys

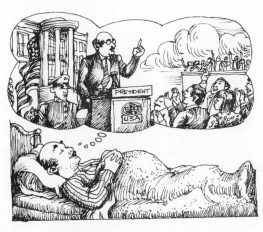

3. Mr. Bascomb

4. Mr. Fix

 LISTENING PRACTICE • *Listen to these people talk about their dreams. What do their dreams reveal about them?*

 CONVERSATION • *Listen and practice.*

BARNEY: I had an incredible dream last night.

FRED: Oh, really? What happened?

BARNEY: I dreamed I was riding in a convertible with Ula Hackey. I was a big Hollywood producer, and Miss Hackey was crazy about me. Everywhere we went, people smiled and waved to us.

PAIR WORK • *Have similar conversations. Make up a dream and tell your partner about it, or talk about a dream you really had. Ask each other questions about your dreams: Where were you? What happened? How did your dream end?*

TALKING ABOUT THE LEGAL SYSTEM

The Fix trial is big news in Wickam City. Everyone has been talking about it.

1. Have you ever watched a trial in a courtroom or on TV?
2. What is the most interesting trial you have seen or heard about?
3. Who was on trial? What was the defendant accused of doing?
4. What was the verdict? Was the defendant innocent or guilty?
5. In your country, do you have jury trials, or does the judge decide?
6. Do juries and judges sometimes find innocent people guilty?
7. Do they ever let guilty people go free?
8. Do you think a rich defendant has a better chance in court than a poor defendant? Why?
9. If you were a lawyer, would you defend someone you knew was guilty?

TALKING ABOUT RENTING APARTMENTS

In Wickam City it is becoming more difficult to find an apartment, and the rents are going up. That is because there are more people looking for apartments, and there are fewer vacancies.

1. Is it easy or difficult to find a nice apartment in your city?
2. What are some of the important considerations in looking for an apartment?
3. How do most people find their apartments?
4. Why is it getting more expensive to rent an apartment nowadays?
5. Do you think rent control is a good idea? Why?
6. Are you living in an apartment now?
7. What are some of the regulations that tenants must observe?

ROLE PLAY

Student A plays the part of a landlord. Student B plays a person who is looking for an apartment.

Situation: The landlord is showing the person an apartment that is for rent. The person wants to know how much the rent is, what the tenants in the building are like, if it is quiet, if the neighborhood is safe, if there is public transportation nearby, and if there is a market within walking distance.

Student A plays a landlord. Student B plays a tenant.

Situation: The landlord criticizes the tenant for not paying the rent on time and for not obeying the rules. The landlord is particularly unhappy about the tenant making too much noise. The tenant complains that there are too many rules, and says that some of them are impossible to obey.

COMPOSITION

1. Describe an interesting dream you had. What do you think was the meaning of your dream?
2. Describe an ideal afternoon. Where did you go? Who were you with? What did you do?

VOCABULARY

absolute	deep (adj.)	gentlemen	obey	violate
accuse	defendant	guilty	once (adv.)	
agent	defense			worthless
apologize	dependable	illegal	percent	
argument	discriminate	improvement	petition (n.)	
audition (n.)	discussion	income		
	dishonest	incredible	regulation	
benefit (v.)	dream (n.)	independent	rule (n.)	
	dream (v.)			
capable		judge (n.)	silence	
celebrate	excuse (n.)		specific	
celebration		landlord		
charge (v.)	fail (v.)	law	tenant	
choose	fairly	legal	terrific	
comply	fantastic	local (adj.)	trial	
condition (n.)	favorable			
consequence	fool (v.)	maintain	unhappiness	
considerate	force (v.)	minor (adj.)	unnecessary	
criticize		miserable		

EXPRESSIONS

The rules are impossible to keep.
The tenants have a right to fair housing.

We'll take him to court.
He'll be sorry when we get through with him.

What can I do for you?
I'm glad to hear you say that.

That makes sense.
That's quite all right.

It was no use.
Help yourself.

to be good at something
to be excited about something
to get tired of something
to get rid of something
to object to something

to be responsible for
to be ashamed of
to be capable of

She called a meeting.
They'll settle their differences.

The trial is over.
Court dismissed.

Miss Hackey is crazy about me.
How romantic!

Don't you see?
That's just it.

once and for all
guest of honor

to break the law
to draw up a petition
to throw someone out
to teach someone a lesson
to deal with someone

to go up (the street)
to go down (the stairs)
to cut off (the electricity)

BE USED TO Affirmative

I'm used to getting up early.
_____ taking the bus.
_____ working hard.

BE USED TO Negative

I'm not used to taking a cold shower.
_____ having a big breakfast.
_____ eating alone.

GERUNDS AFTER PREPOSITIONS

I'm	fond of interested in tired of	counting money. working at the bank. staying at home.

He's	afraid of worried about sorry for	losing his job. getting in trouble. being late.

They're	thinking about planning on looking forward to	selling their house. going to Spain. making new friends.

She	believes in insists on benefits from	eating well. doing the cooking. exercising every day.

VERB + OBJECT + GERUND

I	remember object to don't like	you them him	talking about your family. playing football in the street. using the computer.

BEFORE + GERUND

She took a shower before	she got getting	dressed.

AFTER + GERUND

He went home after	he left leaving	the office.

FOR, BY, WITHOUT + GERUND

He got five dollars	for	cutting the grass.
They found the answer	by	looking in the encyclopedia.
She bought some furniture	without	telling her husband.
You complained about your job	while	doing nothing about it.

Chapter

TOPICS
Leisure activities
Proverbs
Current issues
Problems at work

GRAMMAR
Review

FUNCTIONS
Describing experiences
Making comparisons
Agreeing and disagreeing
Giving reasons
Solving problems
Talking about feelings/emotions
Recommending
Giving opinions

Last Saturday Jimmy and his father went fishing. They got up very early in the morning, before dawn, and drove out to Bear Lake. When they arrived they saw a beautiful sunrise over the lake.

As they were putting their equipment into their small motor boat, Jimmy asked his father a question. "Dad, why is this lake called Bear Lake?"

"Well, Jimmy," said Sam, "a long time ago, when your grandfather was a boy, there were bears living in this forest. And the bears often came to this lake to catch fish."

"I've never even seen a bear, except in the zoo," said Jimmy. "Are they dangerous?"

"They can be dangerous, Jimmy. But you won't see any bears today. There haven't been any bears here since my father's time. People have scared the bears far away from this lake."

They launched the boat onto the calm water. "Let's go to the south end of the lake," said Sam. "That's where everybody usually goes."

"But, Dad, why don't people go up to the north end?"

"I don't know. It's further away, I guess. I've never even been there myself."

"Couldn't you and I go there today? Maybe there are some big fish in places where people don't usually go."

"OK, Jimmy, why not? Let's go."

They started in the direction of the north end. Soon they could no longer see any of the other boats on the lake. They continued until they reached the north end, where trees were casting long, dark shadows over the water. They turned off the motor and listened to the silence.

"Let's start fishing here in the shadows, near the shore," said Sam quietly. "That's where the big fish should be."

It was cold and dark in the shadow, and Jimmy's hands were trembling as he began to fish. But five minutes later he completely forgot about being cold. "Dad!" he said, "I've got one!"

The big fish jumped and splashed in the water. Jimmy held tightly onto his rod, worrying that the line might break.

"Let him get tired, Jimmy," Sam said, smiling. "Don't bring him in too fast!"

Finally the fish began to tire and Jimmy could bring it close to the boat. Sam reached down with the net and lifted it out of the water.

"It's a big one," said Sam. "It must weigh six pounds!"

"It's the biggest one I've ever seen!" Jimmy was very happy.

Sam put the fish in the back of the boat. "This is a good place, Jimmy. Let's see if there are any more fish like this one around here."

They began fishing again, but a long time went by and nothing happened. Jimmy began to feel cold again. "Maybe that was the only fish here, Dad."

"Yes, and maybe it was the king of the north end of Bear Lake."

Just then Jimmy turned around to look at his fish, but the fish was no longer in the back of the boat. "Dad, look!"

Sam turned around and saw Jimmy's fish in the mouth of a huge bear. The bear was standing in the shallow water just behind the boat. With one very quick movement, Sam started the motor and the boat began to speed out of the shadow, splashing water onto the big bear. "Whew!" said Sam, "that was a close call!"

From their safe position out on the lake, Jimmy and his father looked back on the bear. And the bear looked at the two people in the boat.

"He's got my fish, Dad! Now nobody will ever believe I caught one."

They watched as the bear disappeared into the forest with the fish still in its mouth. "And Jimmy," Sam said laughing, "nobody will believe our story about the bear, either!"

The boat moved quickly across the lake toward where the car was parked. "Dad," Jimmy asked, "were you scared?"

"I sure was, son."

"So was I. I don't think I've ever been more afraid in my life."

"It's too bad we didn't bring the camera. That must be the first bear anyone has seen around here since your grandfather's time."

"And I guess this time," Jimmy laughed, "it's the bear who is scaring the people away from the lake!"

STORY QUESTIONS

1. Where did Sam and Jimmy go fishing?
2. What did they see when they arrived at the lake?
3. How did Bear Lake get its name?
4. Where is the best place to catch fish?
5. How big was the fish that Jimmy caught?
6. What happened to the fish?
7. What did Sam do when he saw the bear?
8. What did Sam mean when he said, "That was a close call!"?
9. What did Sam and Jimmy learn from their experience?
10. Would you go fishing at Bear Lake?
11. Have you ever had a close call? When? Where? What happened?
12. What did you learn from your experience?

GROUP WORK • *Find out if anyone in your group has ever had a close call. Get the details. Ask when, where, and how it happened. Share the best story with the class.*

PRACTICE • *Combine the sentences using* **so . . . (that)** *or* **such . . . (that)**.

> She's very intelligent. She passed the exam without studying.
> **She's so intelligent (that) she passed the exam without studying.**
>
> He's a very careful man. He seldom makes mistakes.
> **He's such a careful man (that) he seldom makes mistakes.**

1. He's very ambitious. He'll do anything to succeed.
2. She's very lazy. She won't clean the floor.
3. It's a very unpleasant job. Nobody wants to do it.
4. I was very worried last night. I couldn't sleep.
5. You made a loud noise this morning. Everyone woke up.
6. She's a dangerous driver. It's unsafe to go anywhere with her.
7. Your car is very small. You can park it anywhere.
8. He's a very mysterious man. Nobody knows anything about him.
9. She's a very interesting woman. Everyone wants to meet her.
10. They're very talented. You've got to admire them.

WRITTEN EXERCISE • *Find the opposites and fill in the blanks.*

weakness	relaxed	worthless	defeat
strange	succeed	below	public
loser	boring	support	least

1. victory _defeat_
2. fail _____
3. private _____
4. above _____
5. interesting _____
6. strength _____
7. oppose _____
8. nervous _____
9. most _____
10. winner _____
11. valuable _____
12. familiar _____

PAIR WORK • *Make comparative sentences and give reasons for your opinions.*

> A: **The economy and the environment are both important issues.**
> B: **I think the environment is more important.**
> A: **Why?**
> B: **Because we can't live very well without clean air and water.**
> A: **You're right.** OR **I disagree. I think the economy is more important because our jobs depend on it.**

1. Otis Jackson and Mr. Bascomb are both good candidates for mayor.
2. Politicians and used-car dealers are both dishonest.
3. Sports and politics are both interesting.
4. Money and friendship are both important.
5. Rock music and jazz are both popular.
6. Boxing and bullfighting are both dangerous sports.
7. Driving a public bus and driving a taxi are both hard jobs.
8. English and Spanish are both important languages.
9. Hawaii and Alaska are both good places for vacations.

GROUP WORK • *Choose one subject from the exercise above, such as **rock music** or **friendship**, and try to explain its popularity or importance. List three or four reasons and share them with the class.*

WRITTEN EXERCISE • *Complete the sentences using **will be able to, won't be able to, will have to, won't have to, would rather,** and **might.***

> I've already cleaned the kitchen. You _*won't have to*_ do it.
>
> Nancy is getting better. She _*will be able to*_ leave the hospital soon.

1. If you take lessons, you _____ play the guitar in a few months.

2. I _____ play the piano than play the guitar.

3. Your car is running pretty well, so you _____ repair it.

4. He works on Saturday, so he _____ see the football game.

5. She likes to swim, but she _____ play tennis.

6. If she wants to be a good tennis player, she _____ practice.

7. If they close the park, we _____ have any more picnics.

8. You'd better take your umbrella. It _____ rain.

9. We have plenty of food at home, so we _____ go to the market.

10. If my brother becomes a doctor, he _____ help sick people.

11. If he wants to be a doctor, he _____ study hard.

12. Don't forget your dictionary. You _____ need it.

1. You can't judge a book by its cover.

2. Actions speak louder than words.

3. The way to a man's heart is through his stomach.

4. A bird in the hand is worth two in the bush.

5. Like father, like son.

6. The best things in life are free.

CLASS ACTIVITY • *Discuss the proverbs on this page. Do you agree with these proverbs? Do you have similar proverbs in your country?*

Listen and practice.

A: What's wrong with Mr. Bascomb?

B: He's *annoyed* because his secretary makes a lot of mistakes.

A: He gets *annoyed* easily, doesn't he?

B: I don't know. How would you feel if your secretary made a lot of mistakes?

A: I guess I'd be *annoyed,* too.

PAIR WORK • *Have similar conversations about the people in the pictures below. Give a reason for the way each person is feeling.*

1. Anne/nervous

2. Johnnie/upset

3. Gladys/depressed

4. Mr. Farley/worried

5. Ed/bored

6. Gloria/scared

GROUP WORK • *What would you do in these situations? Find the best solution for each problem.*

• Your secretary makes a lot of mistakes.

A: **What would you do if your secretary made a lot of mistakes?**

B: **I'd have a talk with her.**

C: **I'd give her a month to improve.**

D: **I'd fire her and hire a new secretary.**

• Your boss yells at you.
• You find a fly in your soup.
• No one asks you to dance.
• You can't pay your bills.
• You're bored.
• Someone is following you.

PAIR WORK • *Take turns asking about feelings. Answer with the best words from the box.*

> You lose your job.
> A: **How would you feel if you lost your job?**
> B: **I'd be upset.** OR **I'd feel depressed.**

angry
annoyed
depressed
disappointed
embarrassed
excited
happy
nervous
pleased
scared
upset
worried

1. You win a million dollars in the lottery.
2. Your neighbor comes over every day to borrow something.
3. Your parents tell everyone how wonderful you are.
4. You give a party and only two people come.
5. You're about to make a speech in public for the first time.
6. Someone tells you that you have a beautiful smile.
7. You're having a picnic and it rains.
8. You can't find a job after looking for six months.
9. You come home and find a burglar in your house.

GROUP WORK • *What makes you **nervous, angry, depressed,** and **scared?** Think of situations that make you feel these emotions and discuss them with the group. Find out if the others feel the same.*

WRITTEN EXERCISE 1 • *Complete the following sentences using reflexive pronouns.*

> He works for ___*himself*___ . We introduced ___*ourselves*___ to the lady.

1. Maria painted the kitchen ___*herself*___ .
2. The children can take care of ___*themselves*___ .
3. I like to think of ___*myself*___ as a good person.
4. You're smart people; you can decide for ___*yourselves*___ .
5. Mr. Grubb lives by ___*himself*___ in a small apartment.
6. I looked at ___*myself*___ in the mirror.
7. We helped ___*ourselves*___ to some cake and ice cream.
8. You may have a big appetite, but you could never eat all that food by ___*yourself*___ .

WRITTEN EXERCISE 2 • *Complete the sentences with the prepositions **about, for, in, of, on,** and **to.***

> Jimmy is responsible ___*for*___ taking care of the dog.

1. We're excited _____ meeting your family.
2. They plan _____ staying here _____ a week.
3. Anne is interested _____ becoming a professional singer.
4. She dreams _____ going _____ Hollywood.
5. Johnnie is thinking _____ buying a car.
6. He's tired _____ taking the bus _____ work.
7. Barbara believes _____ getting a lot of exercise.

Listen and practice.

Barney's cousin from Chicago, Alice Rand, has recently arrived in Wickam City. It's her first time in Wickam City, and she is anxious to see the town.

1. "What do people do around here, Barney?"

"Oh, we have a lot of things. Would you like me to show you around?"

"I'd love it."

2. "There's the Silver Dollar Saloon. It's great for country music and square-dancing."

3. "Do you know a good place for shopping? I want to buy some souvenirs and presents."

"Well, there are lots of shops on Main Street. But the best place is the Swap Meet. You can buy anything there."

4. "Do you have to pay the price they ask?"

"Usually. But sometimes you can bargain with them."

5. "I feel like having a cup of coffee. Is there a café around here?"

"Yes. The Old World Café is just around the corner."

6. "This looks like a good place for meeting people."

"It is. The folks who come here are very friendly."

ROLE PLAY • *Have similar conversations. Student A is a visitor from out of town who wants to know the best places for eating, shopping, and having fun. Student B knows the town very well and makes recommendations.*

PRACTICE • *Make sentences using **wish** + **would** or **could**.*

She won't listen to me.	We can't help her.
I wish she would listen to me.	**I wish we could help her.**

1. She won't talk to Peter.
2. They won't come and see us.
3. We can't call them at work.
4. She won't tell us what happened.
5. I can't do anything about it.

6. They won't do their part.
7. We can't count on them.
8. He can't relax and enjoy himself.
9. He won't forget the past.

WRITTEN EXERCISE • *Complete the sentences using **so** + **had to**.*

He forgot to go to class yesterday, *so he had to borrow my notes.*

1. The bank wasn't open when they arrived, _____

2. They couldn't get a loan from the bank, _____

3. They didn't have enough money to eat in an expensive restaurant, _____

4. There was no place to sit when she got on the bus, _____

5. I missed the last bus, _____

6. He lost his old umbrella, _____

7. She couldn't get any help from her family, _____

8. I didn't remember their telephone number, _____

9. There wasn't any food in the refrigerator when we got home, _____

CLASS ACTIVITY 1 • *Talk about the picture. What's happening?*

GROUP WORK 1 • *The city of Blackstone has problems with (1) crime, (2) unemployment, (3) health care, (4) pollution, and (5) public transportation. Which problem do you think is the most serious? the least serious? Why? Share your opinions with the class.*

GROUP WORK 2 • *What are the most important issues people are talking about in your city? Discuss a current issue and give your opinions.*

Useful expressions:

What do you think about . . .	I don't know. It seems to me that . . .
I think we should . . .	We have to do something about . . .
That's a good point.	I disagree. I think . . .
Maybe you're right, but . . .	It isn't necessary because . . .
Don't you think . . .	That's not true.

CLASS ACTIVITY 2 • *Discuss solutions to the most important problems in your city.*

Listen and practice.

ROLE PLAY • *You run into an old friend on the street. You haven't seen each other for a long time. Talk about what you have been doing and make plans to meet again soon. Act out a conversation similar to the one on page 150.*

Here are some alternative questions and answers you can use:

A: **How long has it been?**   B: **Two years, at least.**
                                   OR **Let's see. I think the last time was . . .**

A: **What have you been doing?**   B: **I've been working/studying . . .**
                                   OR **Same thing. I'm still . . .**

A: **Let's meet for a Coke/coffee.**   B: **Sure. Are you free tomorrow?**
                                        OR **Great idea. How about this Friday?**

PRACTICE 1 • *Make questions.*

Gloria made a chocolate cake.
What did she make?

Otis has been on the phone for thirty minutes.
How long has he been on the phone?

I want the new dictionary, not the old one.
Which dictionary do you want?

1. The library is on Main Street.
2. I'll be at the library for two hours.
3. That book belongs to Albert.
4. He didn't go to the party because he had to study.
5. The final exam is on Monday.
6. Barbara and Tino play tennis three times a week.
7. Barbara usually wins.
8. She's been playing tennis for nine years.
9. Maria bought the red dress, not the blue one.
10. She likes to shop at Olson's Department Store.
11. Peter slept seven hours last night.
12. He had ham and eggs for breakfast this morning.

PRACTICE 2 • *Make sentences using . . . promised . . . would.*

I wonder why Nancy hasn't written to me.
She promised she would write to me.

I wonder why the boys didn't do their homework.
They promised they would do their homework.

1. I wonder why Sam hasn't repaired the garage door.
2. I wonder why Mabel didn't make spaghetti for dinner.
3. I wonder why Peter and Maria didn't come to the party.
4. I wonder why Barbara hasn't called me.
5. I wonder why you haven't introduced me to your father.
6. I wonder why the girls didn't wait for us.
7. I wonder why Albert hasn't returned the dictionary.
8. I wonder why Linda didn't attend the meeting.

To err is human. We all make mistakes. But in the business world, we need to be aware of the kinds of mistakes that may prevent us from being successful. Here are a number of business mistakes you may want to avoid:

• **_Making a fashion statement at work._** Follow the written and unwritten dress code at work. Whether you work in a suit-and-tie office or a more casual office environment, learn to go with the flow, and you'll avoid making a fashion mistake.

• **_Bad-mouthing people and complaining about them behind their back._** Bad words have a way of coming back to haunt you. Even if your bad-mouthing and complaints never get back to your boss, you'll probably still get a reputation as a complainer, and your hopes for a brilliant career will be shot down.

• **_Trying to "wing it" at meetings._** Preparation helps to make a meeting run more smoothly. It also shows that you are motivated in what you do. Prepare ahead of time . . . or prepare for disaster.

• **_Forgetting the little things people do for you._** The people around you are human beings like yourself who need to feel appreciated for the things they do. Co-workers whose efforts you brush off as "unimportant" today may become very valuable to you in the future. If you forget to acknowledge the little things these people do for you, they may stop helping you out and start standing in your way to success.

• **_Showing up fashionably late._** Businesspeople are busy and don't have time to wait for you to show up. Lateness is rude and should be avoided at all costs.

• **_Taking a "boring" assignment lightly._** If you're given an assignment you consider to be nothing but "busy work," put your best effort into it anyway. You'll impress your boss with your attitude and your ability to take responsibility seriously.

1. Do you think it's necessary to have a dress code at work? Why?
2. What are some workplaces where a suit and tie are required?
3. What are some businesses that allow their employees to dress casually?
4. Why is bad-mouthing at the workplace a bad idea?
5. Do you know any complainers? What do they complain about?
6. Why is it important to prepare for meetings ahead of time? What happens to people who aren't prepared?
7. Why is it important to show your appreciation for the little things people do for you?
8. Why is it important to be on time for work?
9. Should you give "boring" assignments your best effort? Why?

GROUP WORK • _You have just read about business mistakes that can ruin your career. What do you need to do in order to be successful in business? Make a list of five things you should do and share your ideas with the class._

ROLE PLAY • *Choose one of these situations and make up a conversation. Role play the conversation before the class.*

FREE RESPONSE

1. What have you been doing lately?
2. What are some things you spend a lot of time doing?
3. What are some things other people want you to do?
4. What are some things you wish you could do?
5. Who do you look like in your family?
6. What are your best qualities?
7. When was the last time you bought something for yourself?
8. What will you do if the weather is good this weekend?
9. Would you rather go to the park or see a movie?
10. Where would you go if you could travel anywhere in the world?
11. What would you do if you had more free time?
12. What are some of the things you plan on doing in the near future?

VOCABULARY

amusement park	folks	north	robber	unsafe
	further (adv.)			
bear (n.)		onto	safe	
	heart	over	scare (v.)	
calm (adj.)	huge		shadow	
completely		park (v.)	south	
	judge (v.)	position	souvenir	
dawn (n.)			sunrise	
	mouth	quietly	swap meet	
equipment	movement			
		rob	talented	

EXPRESSIONS

Hey, Sandy!
What a surprise!

What have you been up to?
Let's get together soon.

I'd love it.
Good for you.

I'm getting hungry.
I feel like having coffee.

Thanks for showing me around.
My pleasure.

I haven't seen you for ages.
How time flies.

It was good seeing you again.
Take care.

Whew!
That was a close call!

It's just around the corner.
You haven't seen anything yet.

Did you hear about Mary?
Can't you do anything right?

to be bored
to be scared

to be annoyed
to be depressed

1. She _____ television since she got home a couple of hours ago.
   A. watches
   B. is watching
   C. has been watching
   D. watched

2. Has Nick finished his work yet?

   Yes, he _____ half an hour ago.
   A. has finished
   B. was finishing
   C. finishes
   D. finished

3. The boys were playing football when we _____ the park.
   A. were leaving
   B. left
   C. have left
   D. leave

4. She will make dinner when she _____ home.
   A. gets
   B. gets to
   C. will get
   D. is getting

5. He _____ the rent last Friday.
   A. pays
   B. was paying
   C. has paid
   D. paid

6. I was doing the shopping while you _____ .
   A. have been studying
   B. were studying
   C. studied
   D. study

7. He works hard. So _____ .
   A. does she
   B. she does
   C. is she
   D. works she

8. They don't have much free time. Neither _____ .
   A. do we have
   B. do we
   C. we do
   D. are we

9. I enjoy _____ music.
   A. listen to
   B. listening
   C. listening to
   D. to listen to

10. You will succeed if you _____ .
    A. are trying
    B. will try
    C. try
    D. are going to try

11. She will be late unless she _____ now.
    A. leaves
    B. is leaving
    C. is going to leave
    D. will leave

12. I know a man _____ wife is a taxi driver.
    A. who's
    B. his
    C. the
    D. whose

13. Do you know a good place _____ we can have lunch?
    A. somewhere
    B. where
    C. anywhere
    D. there

14. She was sick. That's _____ she didn't go to work yesterday.
    A. why
    B. when
    C. because
    D. how

15. He kept on _____ the same mistakes.
    A. to make
    B. to do
    C. making
    D. doing

16. You'd better take your umbrella. It _____ rain.
    A. might
    B. must
    C. can
    D. would

17. She looks _____ an actress.
    A. as
    B. as if
    C. like
    D. as though

18. My hat is different _____ yours.
    A. to
    B. as
    C. like
    D. from

19. She _____ take a taxi because she was in a hurry.
    - A. has to
    - B. had to
    - C. must
    - D. should

20. We expect them _____ at nine o'clock.
    - A. are coming
    - B. come
    - C. to come
    - D. will come

21. She would rather read _____ listen to the radio.
    - A. than
    - B. to
    - C. but
    - D. and

22. If I were you, I _____ take the bus.
    - A. shall
    - B. can
    - C. will
    - D. would

23. I wish my car _____ make so much noise.
    - A. won't
    - B. didn't
    - C. can't
    - D. doesn't

24. She plays tennis _____ that everyone thinks she is a professional.
    - A. so good
    - B. too well
    - C. very well
    - D. so well

25. He meets _____ people that he can't remember all their names.
    - A. so many
    - B. so much
    - C. very many
    - D. too many

26. You're an intelligent person and you can take care of _____ .
    - A. you
    - B. your
    - C. yourself
    - D. yourselves

27. If she _____ Peter her telephone number, he would call her.
    - A. gave
    - B. gives
    - C. will give
    - D. has given

28. They _____ raise animals if they lived on a farm.
    - A. shall
    - B. should
    - C. can
    - D. could

29. If he had more time, he _____ take piano lessons.
    - A. can
    - B. will
    - C. would
    - D. may

30. I'm interested _____ getting a job at the airport.
    - A. for
    - B. in
    - C. about
    - D. to

31. She's thinking _____ her house.
    - A. to sell
    - B. about selling
    - C. on selling
    - D. she sell

32. He took a shower before _____ dressed.
    - A. he gets
    - B. to get
    - C. getting
    - D. he has gotten

33. I want to know what _____ .
    - A. are those boys doing
    - B. will those boys do
    - C. were those boys doing
    - D. those boys are doing

34. Do you know where _____ ?
    - A. is the hotel
    - B. can I find the hotel
    - C. was the hotel
    - D. the hotel is

35. He promised that they _____ the following Saturday.
    - A. come
    - B. shall come
    - C. would come
    - D. are coming

36. Don't forget to give him the message when you _____ him.
    - A. see
    - B. will see
    - C. have seen
    - D. are seeing

37. She _____ in Paris since 1968, and she is still there now.

    A. lived   C. is living
    B. has lived   D. lives

38. For the past ten minutes I _____ for my friend to come. He hasn't arrived yet.

    A. wait   C. have been waiting
    B. am waiting   D. waited

39. He would feel better if he _____ more sleep.

    A. got   C. will get
    B. gets   D. has gotten

40. She was crossing the road when she

    _____ the package.

    A. drops   C. was dropping
    B. dropped   D. has dropped

41. There wasn't _____ traffic on that street last night.

    A. many   C. a little
    B. a lot of   D. much

42. We don't have _____ apples.

    A. much   C. some
    B. any   D. few

43. You don't like to exercise, _____ ?

    A. you do   C. you don't
    B. don't you   D. do you

44. I don't know _____ at the bank.

    A. anyone   C. someone
    B. any person   D. nobody

45. He won't be able to finish studying those reports at the office. He wants to

    _____ at home.

    A. look for them   C. look them over
    B. look after them   D. look them up

46. I saw the paintings _____ were in the living room.

    A. that   C. there
    B. who   D. those

47. She isn't _____ to lift that box.

    A. so strong   C. enough strong
    B. very strong   D. strong enough

48. You are the _____ person I've ever known.

    A. luckier   C. most lucky
    B. more lucky   D. luckiest

Circle the letter that shows where the word in parentheses should be placed in the sentence.

49. (always)

    _____ He _____ goes _____ to work _____ on time.
        A   B   C   D

50. (easily)

    _____ She _____ can _____ do it by herself if she wants to _____ .
        A   B   C   D

Appendix

INFINITIVE	PAST TENSE	PAST PARTICIPLE	INFINITIVE	PAST TENSE	PAST PARTICIPLE
be	was/were	been	let	let	let
beat	beat	beaten	lie	lay	lain
become	became	become	light	lit	lit
bet	bet	bet	lose	lost	lost
bite	bit	bitten	make	made	made
break	broke	broken	mean	meant	meant
bring	brought	brought	meet	met	met
build	built	built	put	put	put
buy	bought	bought	quit	quit	quit
catch	caught	caught	read	read	read
choose	chose	chosen	ride	rode	ridden
come	came	come	ring	rang	rung
cost	cost	cost	rise	rose	risen
cut	cut	cut	run	ran	run
deal	dealt	dealt	say	said	said
do	did	done	see	saw	seen
draw	drew	drawn	sell	sold	sold
drink	drank	drunk	send	sent	sent
drive	drove	driven	set	set	set
eat	ate	eaten	shake	shook	shaken
fall	fell	fallen	shine	shone	shone
feed	fed	fed	shoot	shot	shot
feel	felt	felt	shut	shut	shut
fight	fought	fought	sing	sang	sung
find	found	found	sit	sat	sat
fly	flew	flown	sleep	slept	slept
forget	forgot	forgotten	speak	spoke	spoken
get	got	got	spend	spent	spent
give	gave	given	stand	stood	stood
go	went	gone	steal	stole	stolen
grow	grew	grown	strike	struck	struck
hang	hung	hung	swim	swam	swum
have	had	had	take	took	taken
hear	heard	heard	teach	taught	taught
hide	hid	hidden	tear	tore	torn
hit	hit	hit	tell	told	told
hold	held	held	think	thought	thought
hurt	hurt	hurt	throw	threw	thrown
keep	kept	kept	understand	understood	understood
know	knew	known	wake	woke	waked
lay	laid	laid	wear	wore	worn
lead	led	led	win	won	won
leave	left	left	write	wrote	written

ask out = invite someone to do something (go to a show, a meal)
He asked her out to a movie.

be against = oppose
I'm against building a toy factory in City Park.

be back = return
I'm going to the drugstore. I'll be back in fifteen minutes.

be fed up with = be completely bored
I'm fed up with working. I want to have some fun.

be over = be finished
The meeting will be over in a few minutes.

break into = enter illegally, especially by force (a bank, building, house, etc.)
Last month a burglar broke into my apartment and took the TV.

bring up = mention or introduce a subject.
You can bring up the question of child care at the next meeting.

call off = cancel (an event, arrangement, activity)
We had to call off the picnic because of rain.

catch up with = reach (someone who is ahead)
He was walking fast. I had to run to catch up with him.

cheer up = become happier
My sister was feeling depressed, but she cheered up when you invited her to the party.

come up with = think of, produce (an idea, plan, suggestion)
We must come up with a plan to improve the economy.

count on = depend on, rely on (someone)
If you ever need help, you can always count on me.

do without = manage in the absence of a person or thing
I like coffee, but I can do without it.

feel up to = feel strong enough (to do something)
I'm very tired. I don't feel up to playing tennis.

figure out = understand (someone or something) with difficulty
I can't figure out why she married Bill. He has nothing to offer.

fill in = complete (a form, questionnaire)
It took me fifteen minutes to fill in the application form.

find out = discover after making an effort
How did you find out that she was living in Paris?

get away = escape; be free to leave
The police chased the bandit, but he got away.

get away with = do something wrong or illegal without being punished
She always cheats on her exams. I don't know how she gets away with it.

get back = reach home again
We spent the whole day at the beach and didn't get back until after dark.

get over = recover from (an illness, a shock, a disappointment)
I had the flu last week, but I got over it quickly.

get through = finish, complete (some work, a job, a book)
She had a lot of work to do yesterday, but she got through all of it.

give in = stop resisting; surrender
Her boyfriend didn't want to go dancing, but he finally gave in.

give up = stop trying to do something (often because it is too difficult)
He tried to pick some oranges, but he couldn't reach them. So, he gave up.

go ahead = proceed; continue
Go ahead. Don't wait for me.

go away = leave; leave this place
Go away! I don't want to see you!

go on = continue any action
Go on with your story. It's very interesting.

go out = go to a social event (a theater, concert)
She has a lot of friends and goes out a lot.

grow up = become adult
Children grow up very fast nowadays.

hold on = wait (especially on the telephone)
Hold on. I'll be with you in a minute.

hold up = rob
Two gunmen held up the National Bank last week.

leave out = omit
When he filled out the application form, he left out his phone number.

let someone down = disappoint someone (often by breaking a promise or agreement)
You let me down. You promised to help me, but you didn't.

look after = take care of (someone or something)
My neighbor looks after the dog while I'm away.

look forward to = expect with pleasure
We're looking forward to the party next week.

look someone up = visit someone
She looked up her uncle when she was in San Francisco.

look up to = respect; admire
People look up to Dr. Pasto because of his great knowledge.

make up for = compensate for (a mistake, doing or not doing something)
I'm sorry I forgot your birthday, but I'll make it up to you.

move out = leave a house or apartment with one's possessions
Our neighbors moved out of their apartment yesterday.

pick up = get, collect (something or someone)
She picked up a package at the post office.

pick up = give someone a ride in a vehicle
He picked up his girlfriend after work and drove her home.

point out = show; explain
She pointed out that a small car is more practical than a big car.

put off = delay or postpone (doing something until a later time)
Never put off until tomorrow what you can do today.

put something back = return; replace (something)
When you finish looking at the magazines, put them back on the shelf.

put up with = suffer; tolerate (a difficult situation or person)
Our neighbors make a lot of noise, and we have to put up with it.

run into = meet someone by chance
I was on my way home when I ran into an old friend.

run out of = use all of and have none left (money, time, patience)
She ran out of money and had to borrow some from me.

see about = make inquiries or arrangements
We called the travel agency to see about getting a flight to New York.

see off = say good-bye to someone who is going on a trip
I saw my brother off at the airport last Sunday.

stand up for = defend verbally
Her mother criticized her, but her father stood up for her.

take off = remove an article of clothing
It was very hot, so he took off his coat.

take over = become the person or group in charge
He took over the business after his father died.

take up = begin a hobby, sport, or kind of study
Last year she took up stamp collecting, and now it's her favorite pastime.

talk over = discuss a matter with someone else
Whenever he has a problem, he talks it over with his wife.

think over = consider carefully (a problem, offer, situation)
You don't have to make a decision right away. Go home and think it over.

try on = put on (an article of clothing) to see how it fits
She tried on several dresses before finding one she liked.

try out = test
You should try out the computer before buying it.

turn down = refuse, reject (an offer, application, applicant)
He applied for a job at the bank but was turned down.

turn out = result, develop, or end
Don't worry. Everything will turn out all right.

turn up/down = increase/decrease (volume, force, pressure)
Would you please turn down the radio? It's too loud.

wear out = use (something) until it is finished
He has worn out three pairs of shoes in the last year.

work out = find the solution to a problem
We don't have enough money to pay all our expenses, but we'll work things out somehow.

GERUNDS AND INFINITIVES

VERBS FOLLOWED BY GERUND

Subject	Verb	Gerund	
They	enjoyed	watching	the football game.

admit	dislike	mind	risk
avoid	enjoy	miss	save
consider	finish	postpone	stop
debate	imagine	practice	suggest
delay	keep	protest	
discuss	mention	recommend	

VERBS FOLLOWED BY INFINITIVE OR GERUND

Subject	Verb	Gerund	
She	likes	to swim / swimming	in the ocean.

attempt	deserve	love	start
begin	forget	prefer	try
bother	hate	regret	
continue	like	remember	

VERBS FOLLOWED BY OBJECT + INFINITIVE (WITH **TO**)

Subject	Verb	Object	Infinitive (with To)	
I	wanted	him	to clean	the windows.

advise	choose	get	need	teach
allow	convince	help	order	tell
ask	encourage	hire	pay	train
beg	expect	inspire	remind	want
cause	force	invite	send	warn

GERUNDS

VERB AND PREPOSITION FOLLOWED BY GERUND

Subject	Verb + Preposition	Gerund	
We	believe in	helping	our friends.

admit to	care about	forget about	pay for
apologize for	complain about	insist on	plan on
approve of	count on	laugh about	succeed in
argue about	decide against	lie about	talk about/of
ask about	dream about/of	look forward to	think about/of
believe in	feel like	object to	worry about

ADJECTIVE AND PREPOSITION FOLLOWED BY GERUND

Subject	Be	Adjective + Preposition	Gerund	
He	is	afraid of	losing	his job.

afraid of	disappointed about	interested in	sorry about/for
accustomed to	disturbed about	lucky at	surprised at/about
ashamed of	excited about	new at	tired of
bad at	famous for	opposed to	upset about/over
bored with	fast at	proud of	used to
capable of	fond of	responsible for	worried about
careful about	glad about	sad about	
confident of	good at	sick of	
concerned about/with	happy about	slow at	

1. **BARNEY**   I dreamed I was riding in a convertible with Ula Hackey. I was a big Hollywood producer, and Miss Hackey was crazy about me. Everywhere we went, people smiled and waved to us.

2. **GLADYS**   I dreamed that I was the queen of England. I lived in Buckingham Palace, and I could have anything I wanted. I gave fancy parties for my friends, and they all said, "Long live the Queen!"

3. **MR. BASCOMB**   I dreamed that I was president of the United States. I was the most powerful man in the world. I made very wise decisions and gave excellent speeches. All the American people loved me.

4. **MR. FIX**   I dreamed that I was in prison. I was sitting alone in a cold, dark cell. There was nothing to do and no one to talk to. The food was so bad even the rats wouldn't eat it. It was a nightmare!